M⦿TION
LEADERSHIP
IN ACTION

MICHAEL FULLAN

M●TION
LEADERSHIP
IN ACTION

MORE SKINNY
on Becoming
Change Savvy

A JOINT PUBLICATION

CORWIN
A SAGE Company

ONTARIO
PRINCIPALS'
COUNCIL
Exemplary Leadership in Public Education

learningforward

CORWIN
A SAGE Company

FOR INFORMATION:

Corwin

A SAGE Company

2455 Teller Road

Thousand Oaks, California 91320

(800) 233-9936

www.corwin.com

SAGE Publications Ltd.

1 Oliver's Yard

55 City Road

London, EC1Y 1SP

United Kingdom

SAGE Publications India Pvt. Ltd.

B 1/I 1 Mohan Cooperative Industrial Area

Mathura Road, New Delhi 110 044

India

SAGE Publications Asia-Pacific Pte. Ltd.

3 Church Street

#10-04 Samsung Hub

Singapore 049483

Copyright © 2013 by Corwin

Printed in the United States of America

A catalog record of this book is available from the Library of Congress.

ISBN 978-1-4522-5693-1

This book is printed on acid-free paper.

Acquisitions Editor: Arnis Burvikovs

Associate Editor: Desirée A. Bartlett

Editorial Assistant: Kimberly Greenberg

Production Editor: Cassandra Margaret Seibel

Copy Editor: Sarah J. Duffy

Typesetter: C&M Digitals (P) Ltd.

Proofreader: Dennis W. Webb

Indexer: Sylvia Coates

Cover Designer: Scott Van Atta

Permissions Editor: Jennifer Barron

12 13 14 15 16 10 9 8 7 6 5 4 3 2 1

CONTENTS

PREFACE

"Give me the skinny naked truth" was a phrase apparently uttered by a frustrated Colonel in World War II when he couldn't get a straight answer from one of his men. Later it became "What's the skinny?" It means give me the essence of something, the inside dope, not some convoluted or contrived explanation. You need the skinny when something is complex. The skinny is about rendering the complex actionable.

In 2009, when we were immersed in workshops around the world on how to lead change effectively, we realized that what we were trying to get at was just that—the skinny on becoming change savvy. That's what we used as the subtitle of the 2010 book. The main title was *Motion Leadership*—a second powerful concept. It means what it says—what kind of leadership is going to cause positive movement forward in individuals, organizations, and systems. Put another way, how do you motivate the masses, including the gold standard of motivating the unmotivated (and having them thank you afterward)?

A third related concept I borrowed from Jeff Kluger, namely, *simplexity*. As I use it simplexity means that there are a small number of key things you need to know and be good at (the simple part) and then be able to create the chemistry and coherence with large numbers of people that make for effective outcomes (the complex part).

Since the 2010 book our work on leading change continues apace. As usual, I get the best insights from working with and observing practitioners in action. Skinny insights by definition must be sticky, actionable, memorable, and gobsmacking. Such insights have a kind of "why didn't I think of it" and "it seems so right" quality. They give you a blissful sense of clarity, only to be colored by the feeling that I almost have it but maybe not quite. When it comes to dynamic change, shifting conditions, and diverse evolving personalities, the truth is that one can never get settled clarity. The skinny is about working on your clarity and skills on an ongoing basis that gets you as close as humanly possible to leading change effectively. Skinny leaders maximize clarity of action in the face of complex situations while, as we shall see, never being totally sure that they got it right. But never mind, they are learners and get it right more times than not.

A few hundred change stories later, we have more insights on leading change, especially about changing whole systems. You have to be close to the action to pick up these instances of change savvy and to test them against other situations. So now we have *Motion Leadership in Action: More Skinny on Becoming Change Savvy.*

This book builds on work we have been doing in the past decade on "whole-system reform"—how to improve classrooms and schools on a systemwide basis. Over the course of this work I have identified four "wrong" and four "right" policy drivers. By drivers I mean policies and strategies that are supposed to cause wide-scale improvement. The four wrong ones (in the sense that they do not move the system forward) are punitive accountability, individualistic solutions, technology, and ad hoc policies. The corresponding right ones are capacity building, teamwork, pedagogy, and systemic policies. It is not that the wrong drivers have no role to play, but rather that they should not have a front-end dominant role as they do in many jurisdictions, such as the United States. You might ask why a politician would consciously promote an ineffective policy. The short answer is that the policies in question appear to offer a quick fix, and they can be legislated.

By contrast the motion leaders that I feature in this book have mastered the use of right drivers. They all operate in complex environments that contain mixtures of ineffective and effective drivers. They are able to contend with the set, maximize the use of the more powerful drivers, and incorporate the merits of the wrong drivers to support movement in a positive direction. Thus we will be able to see up close how effective motion leaders work in difficult circumstances. The lessons to be learned are clear and substantial.

This book is an invitation and a journey to sharpen your own skinny skills. This is a diet that you are going to like. As we said the first time, no need to bring your trunks or swimming suits, we are going "skinny dipping" once more. Skinny dipping connotes thrill and risk in the service of doing something deeply worthwhile. Jump in!

ACKNOWLEDGMENTS

Skinny to the bone, I am going to keep this brief. It is my fortune to learn from effective leaders around the world. My first thanks go to the seven motion leaders featured in this book and to Fr. Egsgard—the only person in the world who could make trigonometry skinny.

And to a world of others with whom I am working, including Ontario educators; the core team at MFE; the Madcap crowd; colleagues in Alberta, British Columbia, and New Brunswick; system leaders across the United States, in Idaho, California, New York, and more; many more down under in virtually every Australian state; and those from several European countries. I could go on, but my point is "it's a skinny world" out there.

Thanks to Andy Hargreaves, Ben Levin, and Mawi Asgedom for very valuable feedback on the manuscript. To Arnis Burvikovs and the team at Corwin listed at the beginning of this book—we have a wonderful productive relationship that is a joy to experience.

Finally, deep thanks to my personal and professional support system. I am surrounded by people who epitomize quality and who contribute unselfishly to whatever we do. I am forever grateful.

ABOUT THE AUTHOR

Michael Fullan is former dean and professor emeritus at the Ontario Institute for Studies in Education at the University of Toronto. He is currently the special advisor to the premier and minister of education in Ontario, Canada. He holds four honorary doctoral degrees—from the University of Edinburgh in Scotland, Nipissing University in Ontario, the University of Leicester in England, and Duquesne University in the United States.

He is recognized as an international authority on large-scale reform, leadership, and educational change. Michael is engaged in training, consulting, and advising governments around the world. His work is driven by the moral purpose of raising the bar and closing the gap for all students.

He is an innovative thinker who is sought after by institutions, publishers, and international think tanks to present, write, and focus the global educational community on what matters in education in the 21st century.

He is the author of many best-selling books, most recently *Moral Imperative Realized, Motion Leadership, The Challenge of Change, All Systems Go, Putting FACES on the Data* (with Lyn Sharratt), *Change Leader, Professional Capital: Transforming Teaching in Every School* (with Andy Hargreaves), and *Stratosphere*. His books are published in many languages.

Visit his website at www.michaelfullan.ca.

1

NOT-SO-SKINNY CHANGE PROBLEMS

Change challenges abound in the educational world and seem as different as chalk and cheese. But they all have one thing in common: How do you move the seemingly unmovable, and how do you do this on a large scale? We are well beyond accepting that ad hoc successes constitute progress. Small wins don't last.

In many countries, certainly the United States, students are at best increasingly bored as they move through the grades, and teachers are increasingly alienated as they move through their careers. As we say, there is only one thing worse than being bored, and that is having to teach the bored! Even the high-flying countries— Singapore, Korea, Finland—are not doing as well as commonly thought. The now famous PISA assessments of the performance of 15-year-olds in literacy, math, and sciences conducted every second year since 2000 show no absolute gains over the decade since its inception (Organisation for Economic Co-operation and Development, 2010). All systems seem to be running out of gas.

Consequently, leaders are in an action mode. But what should they do? Consider the following range of situations, all of which I know and most of which I have been or am involved in.

What would you do if you were sitting on the newly formed New York City Excellence Commission (2012), whose job it is to influence the change agenda (policies and strategies alike) of the next mayor of New York, to be elected in 2013? You know that New York has gone through almost a decade of tumultuous, highly contested reforms under Chancellor Joel Klein and Mayor Bloomberg. Despite enormous effort, you know that the results have been meager in the big scheme of things. Of the current ninth graders (who were in kindergarten when the current reforms were enacted), only one-third can read, write, and do math on grade level. Half of White and Asian students graduate ready for college (itself a very low figure), compared to just 13% of African American and Latino students, and only 7% of English language learners. You know that the whole affair has been "savaged by Ravitch" and other high-profile researchers with some very strong arguments and precise data, but alas with very few ideas about what to do (see Ravitch, 2010).

As you examine what has happened, you realize that most of the administration's political energy has focused on structural reforms and accountability measures. What's missing is capacity building for all teachers and school leaders and ownership of the reform strategy. But what do you do? The skinny change leader knows that *being right is not a change strategy*. You know that a big price has been paid over the past decade; many New Yorkers—teachers, principals, parents, students, and communities—have become alienated and even hostile to the school system. There have been pockets of great success, but you want all 1,600 schools to be part of a whole system on the move. You are determined that history will not repeat itself. You have only a year to try to shape the next period and influence the next mayor and his or her team. How do you and your fellow commissioners tackle this assignment?

Well, you might start by having a group of leaders, including some of the most likely mayoral candidates, do a study visit to Ontario to examine what education officials did to get successful whole-system reform, province-wide and in the large, diverse urban districts of the city of Toronto and the York Region. But how will you translate these lessons to New York City? How can you adapt and use the now considerable research and evidence on what we call whole-system reform (Fullan, 2010; Levin, 2012b)?

Let's go to London, where we have both great news and challenging news in the borough of Hackney, one of 12 inner-London local authorities. In the year 2000 Hackney was in chaos—a failing, bankrupt system of some 220,000 ethnically diverse people, and just under 100 schools of various types. Hackney's own council advertised for a new chief executive with the following words: "The person appointed would face 'an absence of coherent political leadership, a disconnection between strategy and operation, poor financial management and a lack of focus on basic services" (Boyle & Humphreys, 2012, p. 1). Only the English could make such an offer sound attractive! Even the famed stiff upper lip would be useless in this situation. But Hackney did move, in one decade, to be a highly successful school system, surpassing the national average on student performance and better than many of the richer English school authorities.

We will see in Chapter 2 how Hackney performed this magnificent feat (with many lessons for our motion leader). But we have a new change challenge. The person on the hot seat is Trish

Okoruwa. Trish was a key leader at the school level during the decade of rising success. She was the executive head of a cluster of five schools that helped each other move from "special measures" (England's term for failing schools) to high performance. She then became deputy director of the system.

Today, Trish has a new double whammy. Since 2002 the borough has been run by a so-called Learning Trust that the borough council set up to run the system. In August 2012, by initial agreement the schools returned to the borough to be once again overseen by the council. They have appointed Trish to be the director (superintendent) of the new entity, which has been named Hackney Learning Trust. We will learn later what Hackney did to get such inner-city reform success. Even more interestingly, we will examine how Trish is approaching the new challenge of sustaining and building on a high-profile success.

Back to the United States, in California: At the state level the system lacks focus, money, and any strategy to work with its 1,000 school districts. A few districts, however, have been very successful and want to both sustain what has been achieved and extend help to others. We will take as our example Marc Johnson, who took over Sanger School District in central California a decade ago. His welcome present, so to speak, was the state Department of Education sending him a letter shortly after he started naming Sanger as a failing district.

Sanger is currently an undeniable success as Marc heads for retirement. How did he and his colleagues change the culture and performance of Sanger? What should he do postretirement as a member of a group of eight potentially influential districts that have formed themselves into a group called CORE (California Office to Reform Education): Clovis, Fresno, Long Beach,

Los Angeles, Oakland, Sacramento, San Francisco, and Sanger. We will hear from Marc later.

Take another interesting reform example, Uruguay, a small South American country of 3.3 million people with Brazil to the north and Argentina to the west. Miguel Brechner is the head of a national project called Plan Ceibal that set out 4 years ago to infuse computers into the whole system—one computer per student, and one per teacher (Regional Bureau for Sciences in Latin America and the Caribbean, 2011). Some 450,000 laptops have been distributed since then. Our team in Toronto is at the early stages of describing and assessing the impact of the strategy. Miguel says he wanted to introduce computers throughout the whole system in a manner that "would not complicate the lives of teachers." Certainly sounds like a skinny strategy, but could it be an effective one?

How about down under with Jim Watterston? In 2008 Jim became director general of the state school system in Canberra (Australian Capital Territory). At the time it was a good but stagnant system of some 80 schools with little internal energy and flatlined scores. Our team worked with the territory from the beginning and recently filmed three of its schools and the system leadership. We found great energy and increased performance across the whole system. Jim and his school leaders used the skinny to get there. In Chapter 2 we will see how they did this.

But there is an interesting twist to the situation. Jim took a new position in early 2012 to be deputy secretary of the state of Victoria, a much bigger system, and one that has had a lot of development over the past decade but has not accomplished much focus and coherence on the ground. It shows in the state's performance, as it has not been able to move forward on literacy, numeracy, or other measures of achievement. What is interesting for Jim is that the previous regime did a lot of what looks like the right things (leadership development, capacity building). But it didn't work! What will the new challenge be in Victoria? This is exactly the kind of complex challenge that skinny leaders are cut out to deal with. They know that success in one situation by no means guarantees success in the next one. In Chapter 4 we will see what Victoria is up to as it tries anew for whole-system reform.

Speaking of success in one situation not dictating what should be done in the next one, consider a case of going from New York to California. This lesson of nontransferability was learned the hard way when Tony Alvarado, an excellent change leader, moved in 1997 from New York City to become chancellor of education in the San Diego city school system. Alvarado was one of the very first leaders to bring about successful districtwide reform when he was superintendent of District 2 in New York. From 1987 to 1996 he helped lead the district from 10th and 4th (of 32 districts) in reading and math, respectively, to become 2nd in both subject areas. Alvarado was probably the first successful districtwide reform leader in the modern era.

He learned a lot about change in his first big success, perhaps too much. Because when he applied the ideas—focus on instruction, development and deployment of literacy and math coaches, relentless moral purpose, investment in and insistence on quality leadership at the school and district levels, monitoring of results—to a new culture and a new set of conditions, it backfired. There are many sides to the San Diego story, but it might be that Tony and his boss, Chief Superintendent Alan Bersin, pushed too hard (we will talk about the dynamic duo of push and pull in Chapter 3). They spent a frustrating 7 years (1997–2004) and left more or less together under a cloud of defeat.

San Diego has had a series of superintendents in the last 8 years. The question is not that Alvarado failed, but whether he was influenced too much by his previous successful strategies and whether he could have approached the situation differently. Skinny leadership and context are intimately related. Each new situation calls for new nuanced actions. Skinny leaders have the capacity to be simultaneously humble and confident as they approach each new situation. They know it will be different in key aspects, but their change instincts, or *change stances* as I call them in Chapter 3, will help them figure things out. In other words, change leaders are adaptable in ways that make it more likely that they will be successful across settings.

In Ontario, Canada, what about principal James Bond? (Yes, that's his real name.) James became principal of a small Grade 6–8 school, Park Manor, in Elmira, just west of Toronto. He wanted to integrate pedagogy and technology in order to accelerate learning, but he could find no role models. He and his staff created their own model and strategy and are now rapidly moving to the future. We will look into how they did it.

While we are in Ontario, let's consider the whole province since its education premier, Dalton McGuinty, was first elected in October 2003. I have written about this elsewhere, and Ontario's success is a good example of motion leadership for what we call whole-system reform. Throughout McGuinty's two elected terms of 4 years each (and into his third term), Ontario has substantially improved literacy and numeracy across its 4,000 elementary schools, and graduation rates in its 900 secondary schools. At the big system level, there have been impressive gains—literacy, for example, has increased by over 15% in the elementary schools, and high school graduation has gone from 68% to 82%. Gaps have also been reduced in terms of schools in poverty, English language learners (recent immigrants), and special education students. There are new developments, however. In the summer of 2012, labor issues emerged over a legislated wage freeze imposed on teachers, and McGuinty suddenly resigned on October 15, 2012. So we don't know what will happen to the positive momentum and achievements that have already been accomplished.

But let's look at what we can learn about motion leadership at the district level by examining Hamilton-Wentworth District School Board (HWDSB). John Malloy was an area superintendent in a high-profile, successful school district in Ontario when in 2009 he took the job of director (superintendent) of HWDSB. The district has 48,000 students and 125 schools.

The city of Hamilton, just west of Toronto, historically was the center of the steel industry in Canada. Prior to John's arrival the previous administration had set some of the key conditions for success by pushing for a strong student achievement focus, but the system had not yet established a coordinated effort. The persistent push for the student achievement agenda had been accompanied by increasingly strained management–union relations. School leaders were not clear about how they could achieve success. The central office was seen as hierarchical and bureaucratic. John had a sense of what had to be done, but he also knew that "being right" was not a strategy for change. How did he approach the situation to turn things around? More on this in Chapter 2.

I have just identified seven larger-than-life change problems from four continents. They are different, but they are also similar: They all involve the issue of how to motivate masses of people to put in the effort required to improve difficult situations in order to get major gains in student learning. This is what motion leadership and the skinny are all about. The skinny is deceptive. It's hard, but not as hard as we think. This is what Oliver Wendell Holmes was getting at when he said, "I wouldn't give a fig about simplicity on this side of complexity, but I would give my life for simplicity on the other side of complexity." Skinny leaders come through complexity and land all the wiser. Then they are better, even calm for the next situation. They come to have wisdom, defined so aptly by Pfeffer and Sutton (2006) as "the ability to act with knowledge while doubting what you know" (p. 174).

Although I examine specific individuals and the success of their systems in this book, my goal is much bigger. My colleagues and I have been working on how to realize the moral imperative of educating all students regardless of the starting point. *Realizing* means literally what it says—actual results that raise the bar and close the gap for all subgroups as the overall performance of the system goes up. More than this: we do it on a large scale—*whole-system reform* is our phrase. Not just whole districts (although that, too), but whole regions, states, provinces, and countries.

The key to effective whole-system reform is the action of leaders—motion leaders who by definition mobilize the leadership of others and end up being part of a system that is palpably on the move. We will now take a close look at what these effective motion leaders do to move their organizations and systems forward (Chapter 2). And then we will be able to derive *more skinny* to add to our insights about change leadership (Chapter 3). This knowledge and skill base is increasingly clear, specific, and accessible. If you master it, and be humble knowing that you will need to be always learning, you will do good—on a large scale and for a long time. Jump in, and learn to be a better leader.

2

THE SKINNY
AT WORK

The skinny is brief by definition, but we should not think that it is simple. When you work on the other side of complexity, it means that you have figured out and are continuing to learn how to act in the face of complexity. In a sense such leaders get through the fog of complexity and know how to act. They get to the point where they see more clearly what should be done and continue to tweak and refine their actions based on how the scene plays out.

I am going to pick up in more detail six of the seven challenges that I mentioned in Chapter 1 (New York is still at the early stage). Although I personified each case around one person, motion leaders do not work alone. They know they need the group to change the group. Also, these six cases are noteworthy because five of the six (it's too early to assess Uruguay) have serious degrees of success. If we can find common elements across such different countries and cultures, we will be on to something.

Before starting into the cases, I would like to get the reader into the mood of change motion by introducing an interesting scenario. Andy Hargreaves and I recently published a book called

Professional Capital: Transforming Teaching in Every School (Hargreaves & Fullan, 2012). Andy and I had been engaged in a running debate over the past few years in which I argued that the Ontario reform was a very good example of assertively led whole-system reform that integrated top-down drive with bottom-up partnership. He made the point that the strategy had elements of too much imposition. His best examples were Alberta and Finland, both of which had very good success and had more natural bottom-up support. We will return to these larger issues of whole-system reform in Chapter 4, but at this point my goal is to uncover some of the subtleties of push and pull.

In *Professional Capital* we came to agreement around the concepts of the *push and pull of change*. In our discussions we argued about what was more effective, push or pull, and ended with the obvious conclusion that both are necessary. We were on to our next insight about skinny leadership—push and pull are dynamic, powerful change concepts. For now, let's define *push* as change strategies that create high expectations and pressure on educators to perform; to *pull* is to create the vision and conditions for success that attract and draw in good people to want to be part of the effort. But to say this at a general level is not very helpful.

Andy and I did a series of all-day workshops in five cities in the UK in June 2012. Andy came up with a brilliant exercise stimulated by the BBC reality show *Snog, Marry, Avoid.* Snog means cuddle, flirt, make out with (try explaining it in a workshop!). In the BBC program skimpily dressed and overly made-up wannabe young women (and men) are presented and analyzed by an impersonal voice box called the Personal Overhaul Device (POD). The POD gets opinions from the public as to whether they would like to get to know (snog, marry) or eschew (avoid) the person. Most people select avoid. Then the person goes through a "make-under" process, essentially stripping her of excessive make-up and redressing her to bring out her natural beauty. Now, as you might expect, the response become different—mostly snog and marry. Even the person's family and friends don't recognize her.

In the workshop we present to people the following vignette that comes from Ontario and is contained in the McKinsey report *How the World's Most Improved School Systems Keep Getting Better*:

> In that teacher's first week in the school, two of his colleagues visited him and suggested he use "word walls" because they both found them to be effective. When two weeks later, he had not yet put up the word walls, his colleagues visited him again, this time urging him more strongly to put up the word walls, sitting him down to share why this was the practice in their school and the difference it had made for students. A few weeks later, by then well into the school term, he had still not put up the word walls. His colleagues stopped by again after school, this time simply saying: we are here to put up your word walls and we can help you to plan how to use them. (Mourshed, Chijoke, & Barber, 2010, p. 75)

We ask the participants as individuals to reflect on the passage in terms of how they felt about the approach to change taken by the two colleagues. We asked, would you want to:

- Snog it (flirt with it)—be interested but not too committed yet
- Marry it—be fully committed, embrace it totally
- Avoid it—too ugly, scary, not for you

(Before proceeding, write down your own position and the reasons why you selected your particular response—this will be your first step into the skinny.)

In the workshop we always get a range of responses. We ask people to connect with others who made the same choice (for example, we ask those who selected *marry* to hug themselves and find each other; we ask the avoiders to hold their noses; don't ask what we get the snoggers to do). After the "like groups" discuss their ideas, we draw from the whole audience the pros and cons of each selection.

It is interesting that the participants in the workshop start to see themselves in the vignette. Some leaders, for example, realize that they are pushers and identify with the two teachers who wanted to "help" their new colleague. Others, possibly those who have been on the receiving end of aggressive leaders, see the actions of the two peers as "bullying" a colleague. Others wonder whether doing nothing (i.e., simply leaving the newcomer alone) might be the norm in their school, noting that that may not be what should be done. And so on. The result is that participants begin to reflect on their styles and the relative merits of push and pull.

I hope you see now why the skinny is not straightforward. Motion leaders—those getting positive movement forward—learn to use both push and pull in different combinations depending on the context and the stage of development. Now I need to introduce one other concept as part of our new skinny language: *nudge*. Richard Thaler and Cass Sunstein (2008) wrote a revealing change book *Nudge: Improving Decisions About Health, Wealth, and Happiness.*

Nudge is a change strategy based on the assumption that sometimes the most effective thing to do is to make it easy for people to notice something that might tweak their action. It could be a kind of "push against gently" in order to gain their attention. From a change strategy perspective, nudge says that overt pressure (push) does not work to motivate, and active pulling may also get resistance or be ignored. Nudge is more natural and subtle. For example, I can make the case that mere transparency (making new teaching practices easily observed or just displaying results) often tweaks people into action—a strategy that has the virtue of being voluntary but shaped. Thaler and Sunstein argue that people are in fact "nudge-able" and that we should use this strategy more. Having fruit more openly displayed in cafeterias is an example of a nudge factor suggested by Thaler and Sunstein. To count as a nudge, the intervention must be easy to access, but not impositional. Later on I will argue that while the status quo has an enormous power of inertia, simple, gentle nudge strategies can have major consequences.

In sum, here at the outset, let's have our would-be skinny change agent realize that some combination of push, pull, and nudge is the way to success. The point is not to choose among the three forces, but to value their synergy. The savvy is to learn what combinations are best used in different situations. To understand these ideas we need to get inside actual examples of successful change relative to not-so-skinny problems. And we will do this through six of the cases introduced in Chapter 1. In each case the problems became examples of success through noteworthy motion leadership. In three of the six cases—Hackney, Sanger, and ACT (Australia)—we are going to capture the first period of system-wide success, leaving the future until the last chapter of the book. We return to visit them as each of the three motion leaders starts on a new change chapter. Can they do it a second time?

For now, let's start in London.

HACKNEY

In Hackney we have the two-part case of going first from the bottom of the pack to national recognition as a high-performing inner city district, and now to a challenging future with respect to how they maintain and build on their success. How might the second decade be different than the first?

My thanks to Alan Boyle and Salli Humphreys (2012) for their fine study of Hackney, *A Revolution in a Decade: Ten out of Ten,* from which I draw in this first phase of the reform. In 2000 Hackney was one of the worst-performing local authorities in England.

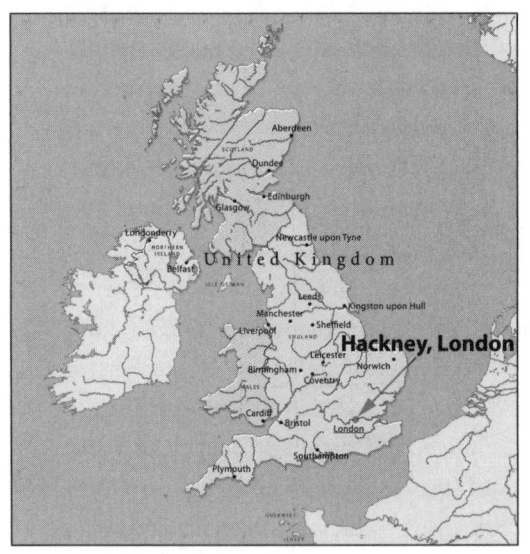

A report at the time from OFSTED (the government inspection agency) drew the following conclusion: "We do not believe that Hackney LEA has the capacity to provide a secure, stable context for continuous educational improvement. The time has come for a radical change" (quoted in Boyle & Humphreys, 2012, p. 12). Somebody went so far as to say that Hackney was the Bates Motel of local government, calling to mind the fatal shower scene in the Hitchcock movie *Psycho.*

We start into the story in 2002, although it could be said that relentless action (not giving up) on the part of the government and the education minister at the time, Estelle Morris, constituted a crucial precondition. In the period 1998–2001 a number of interventions made it clear that Hackney was performing at an unacceptably low level, that high expectations needed to be met, and that outside help and pressure would be used. This "pain before," if we could call it that, was an important part of setting the conditions for further action. The system was simply not going to allow failure to continue unattended. In this sense Hackney become ready for change in a way that it might not have earlier. Incidentally, a similar phenomenon may have happened in Hamilton-Wentworth District School Board. To be more specific, when one sees an example of success it may be worth examining the immediate pre-period, where certain preconditions may be set—relentless expectations, tough slugging to clear some of the way, and so on. What looks like failure to progress in this period may actually be valuable pre-steps to set the conditions for further, more successful action.

In any case, in Hackney in 2002 the borough council created an umbrella organization, the Learning Trust, gave it a 10-year contract, and appointed Sir Mike Tomlinson as chairman and Alan Wood as chief executive. Let's frame the results before asking how they did it.

First, we'll look at the national results in terms of the percentage of students achieving the high standard of Level 4 for 11-year-olds. In 2006, as a baseline measure, 57% of Hackney's students were at Level 4 or above, while the national average was 70%. By 2011 Hackney's students performed above the national average, at 77% compared to 74% (Boyle & Humphreys, 2012, p. 18). Stated another way, they started 13% lower than the national average and 6 years later were outperforming the country by 3%.

The same pattern prevails at secondary school. The standard measure in England is the percentage of students achieving high grades in five or more subjects, including English and math. In 2004 Hackney's students were lagging 10% below the national average (32% vs. 42%). By 2009 they were equal to the national average, where they remained in 2011. In 2002 parents strove to get their kids out of Hackney schools. Today there is a waiting list to get into the same schools. What makes all of these results so dramatic is that at present Hackney is still the most deprived borough in London, and the sixth most deprived in the country.

The Hackney story is one of the judicious combination of push, pull, and persistence. The most powerful examples of this in action are (a) the setting of the highest expectations of everyone's performance for student achievement—a ferocious assertion that failure is unacceptable (a push factor); (b) the investment in leadership capacity by building and utilizing existing leadership, and looking outward for new leaders (both pull and push—the latter included getting rid of leaders who were not suited to the new work); and (c) providing the best possible support for educators to get success (pull). Boyle and Humphreys (2012) call this combination 'the symbiotic relationship between challenge and support which, in turn, drives systemic improvement" (p. 25).

In bringing good leaders together, Hackney forged another of our emerging skinny strategies: *If you want to change something deeply and in reasonably short time frames, you need to use the group to change the group.* The new culture can be expressed in terms of building blocks. You set the expectation and reality that teachers and leaders need to commit to and value learning from each other. Thus individual teachers stop thinking of my students in my classroom, and start thinking of our kids in this school. Individual school leaders become almost as committed to the success of other schools as they do their own. Strong systemwide collaboration becomes the norm as successful schools become willing to share their expertise with other schools, in Hackney's case forming small clusters of federated schools to help leverage the whole system. In a palpable sense, the vast majority of educators come to have a strong sense of *systemness*. They know they are working for the greater good of Hackney, and they take shared pride in doing so.

Trish Okoruwa, whom we will soon cast in a leading role, was a primary school headteacher in the early "bad days." There wasn't any relationship to the system in those days, and there was no guidance: "We had a different slogan every year and a folder would come out with no plan as to how you would actually get there" (quoted in Boyle & Humphreys, 2012, p. 39). Trish also refers to the fine art of push and pull: "There was no question at all [at the beginning] that it was top-down, but it didn't feel that you were being marginalized. . . . There was facilitation to have a dialogue about what it would look like without the blame culture being attached to it" (p. 41). Skinny leaders get away with being pushy because they try to be explicit and avoid creating an accusatory culture. They end up pulling in excellent people who soon become intrinsically committed to the enterprise.

Successful districts also expect—indeed require—that all school leaders have a commitment to the other schools and to the borough as a whole.

Trish Okoruwa, Director, Hackney Learning Trust

I call it establishing a sense of systemness. The chair of the Learning Trust referred to it in these words: "[We] told headteachers that they had to work to the common good: Ok. So you are head of one school but you have a collective responsibility for every young person in Hackney" (quoted in Boyle & Humphreys, 2012, p. 95).

Trish soon became deputy director of the system. She talks about the need at the beginning to combine short-term "find and fix" and long-term "predict and prevent." In other words, when so much is wrong you have to get in there and start fixing, but you also must start to lay the foundation for greater mid- to long-term sustainability. They built their own leaders who would soon enable "predict and prevent" to be the dominant mode.

Finally, Hackney also seems to have resolved the capacity-building accountability dilemma. It blended no-nonsense high expectations; minimal blame culture; support for good leaders; help for struggling leaders and teachers to get better; and then, if necessary, the courage to get rid of those not able or willing to develop further. You know that you are a good motion leader when removing someone is seen as legitimate and peers silently approve the action. Contrast this with current strategies of teacher appraisal whereby the overt front-end purpose is to reward those doing well and fire those at the low end. Without a culture of positive push-and-pull underpinning the effort, this strategy is doomed from the start. Hackney demonstrates that a failing system can set its moral compass high, invest in deep leadership capacity building and support, and cut deadwood when necessary. The fact that this was done sparingly is a testament to the quality of appointments and the responsiveness of those in the posts to rise to the occasion. Push-pull-push, and so on and so forth. Thereby, the whole system rises and moves forward with built-in positive reinforcement.

Now, what is Trish going to do with all this experience and skinny savvy in her new role as director of the Hackney Learning Trust established in August 2012 as the authority returned to the borough council? I interviewed her about this very matter in the summer of 2012. We will get a glimpse of the intended future in the final chapter.

SANGER UNIFIED SCHOOL DISTRICT

Sanger Unified is a sprawling rural district in the central valley of California, just west of Fresno. It's a small district with 10,000 students and less than 20 schools. In 2003 Sanger was designated by the state as a "Program Improvement District" (read: failing district). The number of students at or above proficiency in math and language arts was 31% and 27%, respectively, in 2003–2004. Since then the student population has become ever more concentrated with immigrant English language learners, and with more than 75% on free lunch and 80% minority (mostly Hispanic). During this difficult growth period, by 2008 the district had moved to 59% proficiency in math and 50% in language arts—almost double its previous figures. What happened?

Marc Johnson has been superintendent since the beginning of the reform and

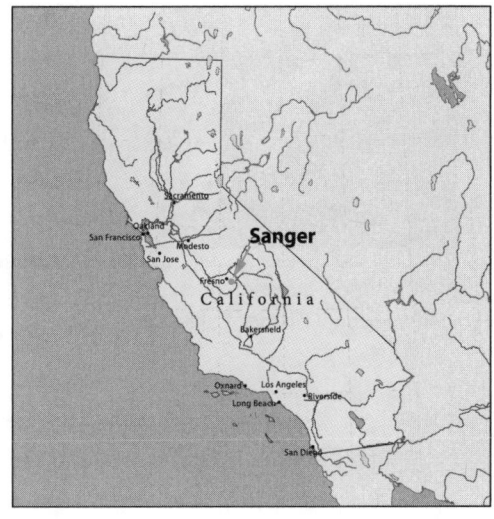

is about to retire in 2013. The flow of improvement has gone like this: First, the Program Improvement designation (classification by the state as a failing district) was treated as a wake-up call (push factor). Second, Marc and his team established from the beginning a strong moral imperative that all kids could learn—no exceptions. There are three core beliefs that everyone now embraces:

1. Hope is not a strategy.
2. Don't blame the kids.
3. It's all about learning.

Marc Johnson, Superintendent, Sanger Unified School District, California

In the early stages this credo is both a push factor (for some) and a pull factor (for others). Eventually it becomes a pull for all.

Third, and like Hackney, Sanger focused on new leadership capacity in all of its schools. The district used professional development to build capacity while reinforcing it by what I would call personnel policies—job descriptions that made it clear that the principal was to be an instructional leader, criteria of appointment to reinforce this, promotion of a new type of principal—and gradual weeding of others.

Fourth, the district developed a small number of priorities and pursued them relentlessly, including literacy (especially ESL) and numeracy.

Fifth, Sanger educators obsessed about implementation. They established a transparent, relatively nonjudgmental data-based system that was founded on the concept of reciprocal accountability, expressed by Marc like this: "If I have an expectation of anyone in the organization, then as a leader I also have the obligation to build the capacity in that individual to meet that expectation" (personal communication, June 2012).

Sixth, the district fostered lots of what we call "learning is the work": creating multiple learning communities (e.g., all schools are in clusters of three or four with focused learning priorities), monitoring data and school plans in order to make corrections, balancing central direction and school autonomy, and seeking new information outside the district by networking with other schools.

In one sense, Hackney in inner London and Sanger in a California valley are as different as chalk and cheese. But examine the strategies. A very small number of elements are at work: fierce moral imperative, relentless pursuit, leadership capacity, instructional focus, and up-close monitoring and learning. What makes it all doable is the building of widespread ownership and shared commitment to help each other.

Many hands do make light work if the hands are coordinated. It is simplexity again, with a very small number of definable factors (simple) and the wonderful but messy orchestration of these factors to create the chemistry required for progress (complex). It's an impressive but also a dynamic balancing act—these leaders know that you can never take the process for granted. It requires constant attention and cultivation.

So Marc now has a double problem: How will Sanger continue to grow after he leaves? Soon not to be his direct concern, but all motion leaders worry about and try to build a legacy for the moral imperative work that they and their colleagues started. There is another interesting question for change leaders who are leaving one system and are still young enough to make other contributions: How can they extend their influence to help others and make a wider impact? In Chapter 4 we will catch up to CORE, the group of eight California districts that have formed a consortium to work together.

AUSTRALIAN CAPITAL TERRITORY (ACT)

In 2008 Jim Watterston left the education system in the state of Victoria (where he had been a regional director) to become director of the Department of Education and Training, the state's education system in Canberra, ACT. Before he arrived on the scene, he asked if I would advise and work with him. ACT was known to be a good system, but somewhat stagnant and definitely not on the move.

ACT is one of eight states in Australia. Each state is constitutionally autonomous in education. The federal government plays an increasingly strong role in standards and performance, especially

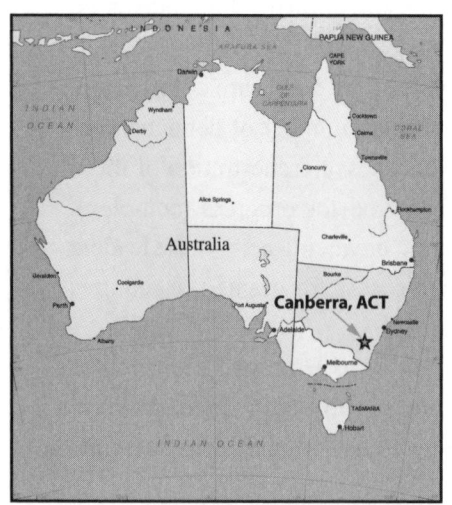

in literacy and numeracy, with the National Assessment Plan for Literacy and Numeracy. ACT has 39,000 students in 84 schools.

We began working with Jim as he was arriving. I should say in all of the successful external consultancies we have been engaged in, it is always the internal leadership that leads and causes the success. It is not our advice that makes the difference but what leaders do to convert the ideas into strategies that fit the context.

We gave Jim the emerging advice from our work in Ontario and elsewhere on whole-system reform. There were eight factors to be considered and integrated.

1. Relentless focused leadership from the center
2. A small number of ambitious goals
3. A positive stance in working with schools and educators
4. A core strategy of capacity building with instruction as the focus
5. Establishing a strong user-friendly database that would transparently serve both improvement and accountability functions
6. A nonpunitive approach to the use of data
7. Learning from implementation during implementation across schools
8. Developing leadership capacity at all levels to foster a sense of systemness and high performance

We also committed to conducting capacity-building sessions for school leadership teams and for system leaders; these were led by my colleague Lyn Sharratt and me. In order to enable focus, Jim decided that he would need to reorganize (we do warn against restructuring unless it is essential, as it often becomes a distracter). The new structure consisted of four clusters of about 20 schools each led by a new network leader.

The group—the central leaders and the newly appointed four cluster leaders—then set out to focus on capacity building, instruction, and the improvement of student learning. ACT's six core principles provide a good rendition of the skinny applied to the system as a whole:

1. Every principal is the instructional leader in his or her own school.

2. Every student will be taught by highly effective teachers.

3. Improving teacher capacity is the most effective way to improve student performance. The strategy of choice is in-class support through coaching.

4. Every teacher and school leader deserves purposeful and regular feedback through high-quality performance and development processes.

5. There is strength in collaboration. As a team, educators will take responsibility for each other's work.

6. Everyone matters. They will do whatever it takes to ensure every young person can learn and thrive in their schools.

Jim Watterston, former Director General, Australian Capital Territory; currently Deputy Secretary, Victoria Department of Education

This should be starting to sound familiar for our motion leaders, but let's look more closely. ACT began to build a performance and development culture in every school. Teachers and school leaders regularly work together to identify, assess, and share the most effective instructional practices and learn from each other in order to increase the collective capacity of their school and network.

Through networks, principals are engaged in observation and coaching to analyze classroom practice, develop and lead whole-school strategies, and provide constructive feedback. A small central team supports schools and network leaders by assisting with the development of consistent understandings to literacy and numeracy assessment and instruction and ensuring that effective practices are shared across schools and networks.

The results in ACT schools were fairly good to begin with because of the nature of their population, but there were pockets of low performance that were left unattended, and these schools were steadily losing enrollment to private schools. Three years later the trend of losing enrollment has been reversed, and the learning of subgroups is on the rise.

In late 2011 we filmed three of the schools (primary, high school, and college [senior high school]) and the central leadership. The resulting four video clips (of about 10 minutes each) make it crystal clear that focus and energy at the school, network, and system levels are very high (see www.michaelfullan.ca). Instruction has improved, focused collaboration within and across schools is widespread, and real progress in student learning is evident.

Given the push-and-pull duo that we are using for motion leadership, it was particularly insightful how the deputy principal of the high school we filmed responded to a question I asked him. We had noticed a great deal of classroom observation and feedback by trained coaches using a quality-teaching framework. We noted that 3 years ago such a practice had been nonexistent and now everyone was engaged in it. He described how some teachers had been wary at the beginning of the process, but more and more joined in as it became clear that the feedback was to be used for improvement. I then asked whether the practice was voluntary or mandatory. His response was one of the best push-pull integration statements that I have heard. He said, "It is voluntary but inevitable"!

Of course, now that Jim Watterston, the director general, has departed for another post, it will be a significant question as to whether ACT will continue in its improvement trajectory. But that's a change story for another time.

HAMILTON-WENTWORTH DISTRICT SCHOOL BOARD (HWDSB)

I mentioned in Chapter 1 that John Malloy became director (superintendent) of HWDSB in 2009, coming from a highly success-

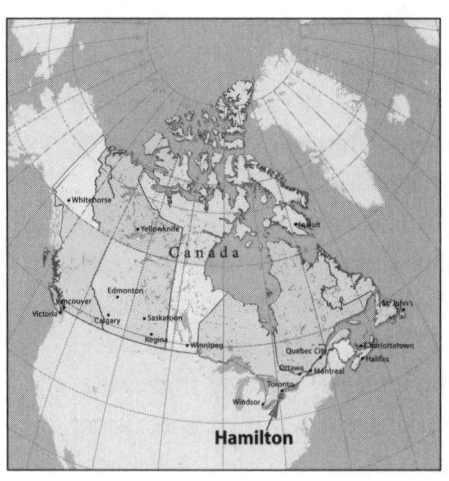

ful multicultural district (York Region District School Board), which we had worked with and written about before. HWDSB was different. In much the way that "the pain before" in Hackney created some necessary preconditions for change, the previous administration in HWDSB had pushed for high expectations and needed improvements.

Still, the system felt overly bureaucratized to many school leaders, there were strained union–management relationships, and there was not a sustained focus on instruction and achievement. Like all of our motion leaders, John started with the existing context. His goal was to build capacity, ownership focus, and clarity: "My first task was to listen. I visited every school and department and asked the same question: What are you proud of in HWDSB, what are you concerned about, and what suggestions or insights for improvement would you like to offer" (personal communication, July 2012).

What he found was that many staff were discouraged about their efforts because student achievement had not improved despite their hard work and the availability of generous financial resources. We often find that schools and districts appear to be, and think they are, doing the right things (valuing moral purpose, investing in capacity building, etc.), but they are not getting anywhere. Having the right elements is not sufficient. These components must be integrated in a way that is focused and cohesive. They must be deeply implemented in practice. It takes many motion leaders to get the chemistry right. There is, in other words, a fine but definite line between having some of the right components in place versus making these factors gel in practice. Put another way, systems strive for alignment by trying to get structures and plans right, whereas the deeper solution requires shared coherence on the part of implementers. *Alignment is about structures, while coherence is about mind-sets.* Motion leaders have a knack for mobilizing new mind-sets.

John also found that many staff felt there was too much pressure and not enough support. Even tools that were very helpful in other districts, such as the province's School Effectiveness Framework, were experienced as symbols of compliance and evaluation rather than professional learning. This is another finding that rings true across situations, namely, that the same tool can be experienced negatively in one place and positively in another. The variable is the context or culture, not the tool. Put a high-quality tool in a negative culture, and you will get increased alienation (because it feels like evaluation in low-trust situations), whereas the same instrument is used as a powerful element of improvement in another situation. *A tool is only as good as the mind-set using it.* As someone once said, a fool with a tool is still a fool.

John Malloy, Director of Hamilton-Wentworth District School Board, Ontario, Canada

John found that, by and large, staff experienced the district as hierarchical and bureaucratic, in which collaboration and colearning were limited and people were frustrated by the combination of working hard and not getting anywhere. Another motion leadership phenomenon: When people are working hard and not progressing, it feels like tough de-energizing work. In cases in which the system is on the move, people are spending just as much time, indeed more time, but it is energizing more than tiring.

John finished his initial data collection with this observation: "Wherever I went, I met dedicated educators who wanted to serve their students well, but they needed a system that would provide more clarity, coherence, and support" (personal communication, July 2012).

This is a classic motion leadership challenge. How do you motivate the unmotivated and discouraged? How do you generate positive movement that will produce new and better experiences and results? John believed in the power of high expectations, but he knew that lofty mission statements were a dime a dozen. Motion leaders have to make things actually happen. He then set out to increase purposeful interaction in the system around a focus he called "academic optimism." He wanted a brief but focused plan (more about the critical importance of "skinny plans" in Chapter 3).

In a nutshell John said, "We clarified and modeled optimism, the conditions that promoted 'Academic Optimism,' and made them explicit every chance we got." In examining what this looks like in practice, it is revealing that the most direct or logical route is not necessarily the best change stance to take. When it comes to push, pull, and shove—indirect (but relentlessly purposeful) is often the best pathway to increased performance. For example, in the previous regime HWDSB set directions by looking at system-level student achievement data, determining improvement goals, and then conveying multiple expectations to schools. This approach, as I said, probably set the preconditions for subsequent success, but it resulted in a plan that was disconnected for many implementers. Says John, "most leaders in HWDSB now admit that they seldom understood or paid attention to what was in the document."

Focus and engagement are two big change challenges for large systems like HWDSB. What John and his colleagues did was to frame the direction around academic optimism, and then, unlike in the past, each school was expected to engage in an inquiry process that self-directs their goals within system parameters. As a common organizer they used the concept of *knowing:* knowing your students, knowing your staff, and knowing your parents and community. It is these simple but powerful keys to connecting to individuals that can make such a big difference. The term *knowing* resonates with the concept I used in my first book, *The Meaning of Educational Change* (Fullan, 1982). Early in my career, as the concept of implementation was beginning to attract reformers' attention, I realized that implementation stands or falls on whether individual implementers find meaning in any innovations that come along. Therefore, strategies should be judged on the degree to which they generate widespread meaning (today we would add capacity as a twin to meaning and add that *shared meaning* is essential for organizational change).

HWDSB's processes to get at deep knowing is clearly a meaning-making proposition. Each school team participates in a self-assessment process whereby they collaboratively analyze student work and data to arrive at the student's greatest learning needs (knowing your students). Then, using the district's School Effectiveness Framework, school teams zero in on a high-yield instructional strategy that will enhance student learning and inform teacher learning in order to accomplish new goals (knowing our staff). This work informs the school improvement plan. Because the school needs to keep refining the work to meet the needs of particular students, each school carries out an action research project that engages parents and guardians of students who are not achieving well (knowing our parents and communities).

The purpose of the action research is to invite parents as partners to work with the school in order to improve their children's achievement, to listen to parents, to teach them about what is being done in schools, and to enlist them in what they can do at home to improve student learning and well-being.

The system is also heavily engaged in new capacity development. It has made a commitment to colearning at every level of the organization. No matter what the role—superintendents, principals, vice principals, instructional coaches, support staff— everyone is expected to be involved in a collaborative inquiry process focusing on changing practice so that students learn better. Says John Malloy, "We are monitoring progress in a supportive way, always focusing on our students, their learning needs, and the learning needs of our staff" (personal communication, July 2012).

There is a lot going on here, but when you look closely the strategy is based on only a few things: focus, engagement, relative autonomy, and coherence (at both the individual and system levels). It is simplexity—keep it confined to a few critical, relentlessly pursued elements (the simple part), and work away on the chemistry of coherence (the complex part).

HWDSB's one-page *Annual Operating Plan, 2012–2013* is a model of simplexity. It contains only nine cells in a 3 × 3 matrix. Down the left-hand side are the three *knowings* (students, staff, parents and community). Along the top are areas of focus, strategies and processes, and indicators of progress.

The plan was built over a 2-year period with widespread participation at all levels. When the draft document was presented at a meeting of system leaders (central office and school leaders), there was a standing ovation. Schools could focus deeply on instruction without being distracted by a long to-do list.

In large systems there is always a fine line between individual school autonomy and system coherence. All our successful systems combine school leeway with system direction, clear expectations, and supportive intervention, including aligning resources to needs. When leaders integrate top-down and bottom-up forces, they create a conspicuous sense of systemness. We have seen this time and again in successful districts and states. *Mutual allegiance* becomes evident, whereby more and more people enlarge their sense of identity and become committed to the success of their colleagues and the system as a whole. At the same time a curious presence of *collaborative competition* arises, with people saying, "We can do better than last year. We can do better than other schools." But this is not a win/lose approach; it is a kind of friendly competition that I have called *moral olympics,* where there is literally no ceiling on what can be accomplished.

Motion leaders often come up with neat, sticky micro strategies. Two of these in HWDSB are the *impostor syndrome* and the *activity trap.* Concerning the former, we all know that being open about mistakes and what you don't know is essential to learning new things, but it is extremely hard to establish this as a norm. Stating it as a goal is not nearly sufficient, so John Malloy gets at it indirectly by introducing the grabbing concept of the impostor syndrome—not knowing something you should know and finding ways to cover up. John gave an example at an open system leader meeting. When he was a Grade 10 English teacher, he felt foolish because he didn't know how to teach a student to read if a nonreader arrived at his class. It seemed odd to him that an English teacher did not know how to teach reading. So he covered it up. (He now says he learned how to teach reading.)

Then an elementary school principal offered his example. Implementing junior and senior kindergarten is now a provincial priority, but as a former middle grades teacher, he had no concept as to what an effective kindergarten classroom should look like. Once you are open about the impostor in you, you can learn more easily what you need to know.

In both instances the point is that we may not know something that is important for our students, our staff, our school, and so on. Because people think we should know it, we don't ask for help, which means we never learn what is needed and we pretend we understand. The solution is very consistent with recent findings by Vivianne Robinson (2011) and others that principals are most effective when they *participate as learners* with staff in figuring out new directions. When they do this year after year, they become more and more of an expert. If you maintain an impostor syndrome, you will never get to be the expert.

Another handy device that HWDSB uses routinely in its discussions is the activity trap. Because relentless focus in the face of multiple distractions is a perennial problem for education systems, a simple gimmick that can be used as a new temptation comes along is to stop and ask yourself, "Is this essential to our core work, or does it take us away from it?" The activities in question are problematic not because they lack value but because they consume energy. This is what Doug Reeves (2011) has called "the law of initiative fatigue" (p. 1).

HWDSB has gained its focus within 3 years, and this is a great accomplishment. If you were a principal in that system in 2008, you likely would not have thought it was possible to get the system aligned. But educators in this district did it in fairly short order. The student achievement results, after being flatlined for several years, have begun to move. From 2011 to 2012, Grade 3 reading and writing increased from 56% and 61% (on the province's high standard proficiency assessment) to

61% and 71%, respectively. Reading and writing in Grade 6 also increased by more than 5% (math is flatlined in the province).

These are not huge gains, but they are significant for a system of some 100 elementary schools to get its act together in such a short time. The system focus and coherence in HWDSB is still an early work in progress. It will be one system on the move that we should keep our eye on.

What about Uruguay, with its curious digital strategy: "We want ubiquitous technology but don't want to complicate the lives of teachers." Huh?

URUGUAY

In 2008 the president of Uruguay introduced Plan Ceibal, a national initiative that is introducing one computer per teacher and one per student ("1 to 1") in all primary and secondary schools in the country. Uruguay has about 2,300 primary schools and 350 secondary schools, including private schools. The population of the country is about 3.3 million.

Since 2007, over 570,000 computers (XOs, a type of subnotebook, and laptops) have been delivered to primary school students and teachers, and to 3 years of secondary and technical schools (Grades 7–9), at low cost (approximately $100 per student), which includes maintenance, Internet access, and initial technical training.

The overall objective is to focus on social equity by universalizing access and use of new technologies. Technical support and networking are offered for teachers, students, and families. An evaluation in 2009 showed that there is indeed widespread access and use of computers across all classes, including family-oriented training, especially for the poor (Martinez, Diaz, & Aloso, 2009). There has been no assessment of the quality and use, and the 2009 evaluation noted that there were concerns with respect to non-educational and recreational use, and lack of access for many poor students (due to damaged, unrepaired computers).

There are various plans for expanding support, including robotics classes, mobile science, online evaluation, kindergarten, math olympics, teacher training, and an updated repair system. The goal was to flood the system with access and technical support in order to get widespread participation as a precondition to accelerate the improvement of learning.

It is thus too early to tell what the learning impact may be. Was the head of the project, Miguel Brechner, right when he thought that an initial low-key approach—get computers out there, but don't try to

Miguel Brechner, Director, Plan Ceibal, Uruguay

directly change teachers—was the way to go? Does Miguel worry when he sees the assessment of neighboring Peru, which 5 years ago launched a one-laptop-per-child scheme for 800,000 school children? Two hundred million dollars later, evaluators note that there is little evidence of impact, that "magical thinking" that technology will do good is "categorically disprove[n]," and that the move may have inadvertently widened the gap between richer and poorer families (Bajak, 2012, para. 13). Should Miguel use a more direct set of interventions at this stage? And how should he combine push and pull? My team (consisting of Nancy Watson, Steve Anderson, and myself) is currently assessing the initiative for the government of Uruguay and has been charged with making recommendations for strengthening instructional and achievement outcomes.

Our interest in motion leadership is how might we think of this initiative as a whole-system reform strategy. It is in this light that Ceibal becomes intriguing. When one is faced with a large problem and limited resources, and a goal of affecting the whole system, what might be the best starting point? In the old days we might have conducted a pilot study, examined the results, and then tried to go to scale. This strategy has a poor track record: By the time the pilot is completed, new priorities have gained ascendancy; there is no money to expand; what has been learned does not necessarily apply to others; and even if the results are encouraging, people in the larger system have no ownership or knowledge of how the success works. If your goal is whole-system reform and you have limited resources, it might be better to use a reflective *ready, fire, aim* approach. Get things started in a way that is widespread but not too disruptive, learn from the start and refine the subsequent stage, create expertise and ownership as you go, and use growing expertise to support other implementers.

Such an approach may be especially suited to the rapid spread of technology, which itself is changing as we use it. In my book *Stratosphere* (Fullan, 2013) I use the metaphors of disruptive innovations and lean startups to examine how technology, pedagogy (instruction), and change knowledge (what it takes to get widespread implementation) might be best integrated. When Clayton Christensen introduced the concept of disruptive innovations, he basically said when something is new and potentially better, the first versions will be inferior examples. This new direction thereby begins an improvement cycle during which many people are working on new developments and adaptations. If we add lean startup strategies, these new developments are rapid and best take place in close interaction with "customers"—in Ceibal's case, with educators, students, and parents. In other words, you need a learning and dissemination strategy as you go.

We can't answer the question of whether Ceibal is on the right track, but we can speculate by putting on our skinny, motion leadership cap. In the words of this book, Miguel and his colleagues are so far primarily using, almost in sequence, a *nudge* and *pull* combination. The mere ubiquitous presence of computers is a quintessential nudge phenomenon (we don't want to complicate the lives of teachers; we are not demanding or evaluating fidelity of use). Once use becomes more widespread, networking is added (a pull strategy) so that implementers learn from each other. Then you might *push* for quality use and focus on laggards. All of this might take place over 5–8 years so that by 2013 you have ever-increasing quality use that has an impact on the performance of students in the country as a whole.

Miguel has some interesting ideas about the dos and don'ts of system change. He observes that if you try to introduce a big change in education, in society it often results in long debates, polarization, and deepening conflict to the point that nothing gets done. But if, on the other hand, you introduce change on a widespread basis but don't insist on particular implementation, if you convey that teachers are essential to any solution, if you listen carefully, if you are relatively firm about the effective ideas you are discovering, and if you look people in the eyes about the moral imperative and best practices, you have a good chance of getting somewhere. He says you have to be firm and tender at the same time, an idea that comes very close to our notion of *impressive empathy* (see Chapter 3).

Our own assessment of Ceibal involves addressing the following questions:

1. How can Ceibal at the next stage contribute to the improvement of learning? What actions have to be taken so that students develop skills for the 21st century, including math and literacy?

2. How can Ceibal promote the collective work of teachers? How can school leaders transform themselves into leaders who use technology and work with teachers and help create the new pedagogy of students as partners in learning?

3. Can Plan Ceibal contribute to the development of systemic and integral policies that establish a directive and supportive infrastructure for whole-system improvement?

4. What concrete goals should Plan Ceibal adopt for the next 5 years to address Questions 1–3?

Once you state the goals this way, you might as well be in Hamilton or Hackney as in Montevideo! And speaking of technology, let us turn to our final example—accelerating learning through integrating technology, pedagogy, and change knowledge.

PARK MANOR PUBLIC SCHOOL

James Bond wasn't always 007. In fact, when it came to technology he and his colleagues were 000 in 2009 (I promise that this is the first and last James Bond joke, but that is the name of the principal). Park Manor is a senior public school (Grades 6–8) with 300 students in the town of Elmira, west of Toronto. I don't usu- 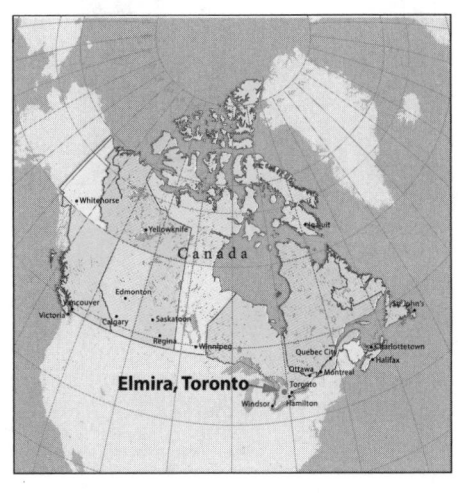 ally write about individual schools in isolation (because a key principle of motion leadership is multiple schools moving, or system change), but Park Manor is one of the few examples of an ordinary school becoming technologically dynamic in a short period of time. And a reminder once more: Although I am personifying motion leadership around a specific individual, all such leaders if they are to be successful mobilize leadership throughout the staff. It is principal James Bond, lead teacher Liz Anderson, and the whole staff ensemble at Park Manor who deserve the credit.

James Bond, Principal, Park Manor
Public School, Elmira, Ontario

When James started as principal in September 2009, the school had two data projectors, an old computer lab, and no technology integration in the classrooms. As of June 2012, the entire school is wireless and every one of the 16 classrooms has a document camera and an HD data projector; half have SMART boards; there are 104 PlayBooks; and the computer lab has 36 new dual-boot iMacs. Pedagogical practice has changed dramatically, teachers are engaged in purposeful learning, and student learning is thriving. What's the skinny here?

In a nutshell, Park Manor's success is built on three key change drivers. One places the moral imperative and pedagogy in the driver's seat; a second is to make technology nonthreatening to use—to treat it as an opportunity to learn new things where mistakes will be normal; and the third is to set up means for teachers and students to learn from each other during implementation. The whole idea is to minimize judgmentalism so that people can learn, a kind of attitude that says, "I don't want to complicate the lives of teachers; I want to enliven them." Learning is voluntary but inevitable!

First, let's establish the pedagogical focus. The school has developed an Accelerated Learning Framework, reproduced here as Exhibit 2.1.

Exhibit 2.1   Accelerated Learning Framework: Park Manor

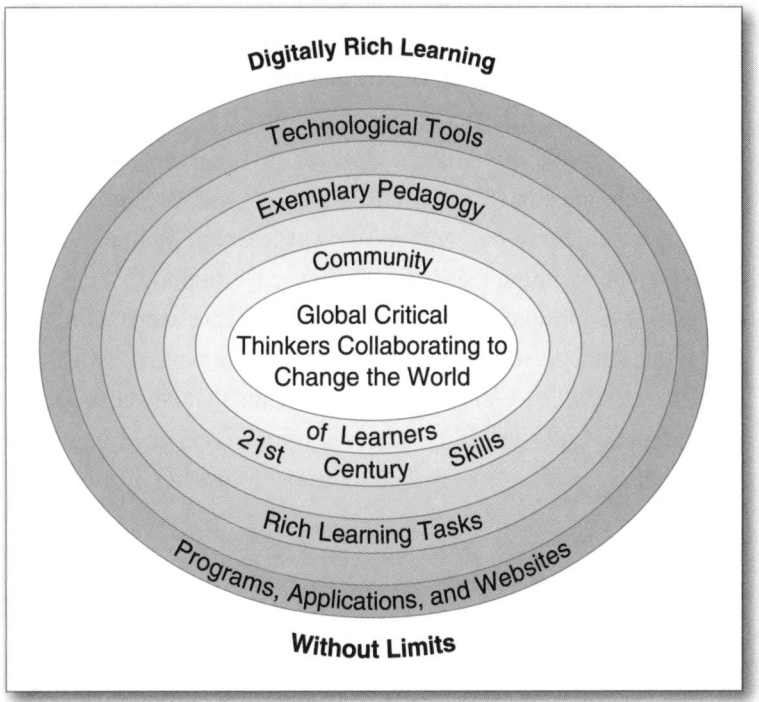

In the center of the framework are the specific goals and success criteria that pertain to global critical thinkers (communication, critical thinking, problem solving, teamwork, citizenship). The success criteria explain in detail how students and teachers can determine that technology, tools, and applications add value to student learning. These criteria pertain to student engagement, active learning, easier learning, assessment for learning (student feedback), assessment as learning (students monitoring their own learning), assessment of learning (concrete evidence), and so on.

Thus the success criteria are linked to evidence of accomplishments (what success looks and sounds like; what students are doing, saying, and producing). In the course of using this framework, the school assesses how much accelerated learning is occurring as a result of particular technologies. Does the technology in question enable the student to *meet* (M) the success criteria? Does it help the student get there *faster* (F)? And does it assist the student in achieving *higher levels* (H) of learning than might have been the case without using the particular technology?

Park Manor, like other successful schools we work with, uses techniques that *personalize progress for each and every student* and does so with *full transparency* for all students that all staff process. For every student in the school, there is a simple one-page diagnostic sheet called a Sticky Note that contains the following information:

Student's Name

Learning Problem

Why Analysis

Root Cause (e.g., engagement, skills)

Countermeasure

Verification (Did the intervention work?)

(See Exhibit 2.2.)

Students, all of them, are then tracked according to progress (color coded) for all teachers to see and learn from. Lyn Sharratt and I call this "putting the faces on data," and if you visit Park Manor you will see data walls galore—very specific, very much living action mechanisms to make and track progress (see Fullan, 2013; Sharratt & Fullan, 2012). All of this pays off. Teachers are excited, students are engaged, and test scores have risen dramatically (although attributing specific causal relationships is difficult). The gains as measured by Ontario's assessment agency have been substantial. The number of students achieving Levels 3 and 4 (standards that reflect higher-order skills) in writing, for example, increased from 49% to 82% from 2008 to 2012. Stated even more dramatically, in 2008 Park Manor was 15% below the school district average (49% vs. 64%); by 2012 it was 9% above the district average (82% vs. 73%). While the trends started prior to the technology infusion, I would suggest progress was strongly leveraged by the integration of pedagogy and technology in the past 2 years. We should also realize that this initiative is still very much at the beginning—less than 3 years old.

Exhibit 2.2 Sticky Note Example

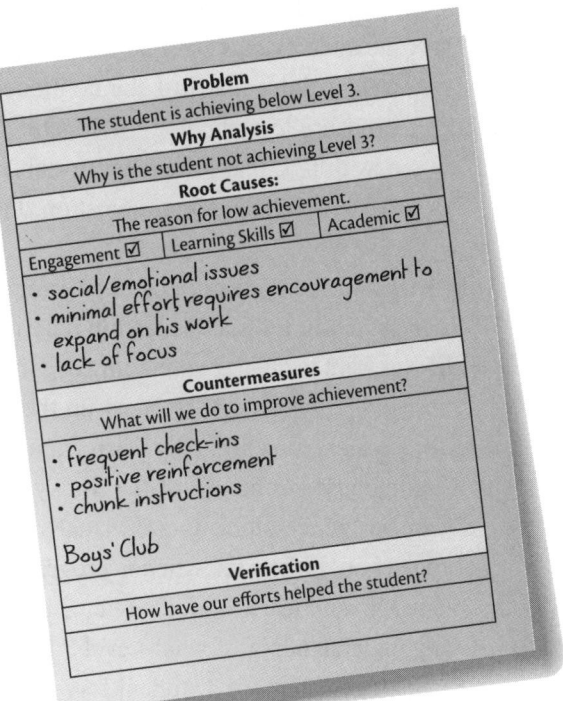

The more interesting motion leadership story is how the school did this in such a short period of time and without the normal change resistance. One of the teachers put it this way:

> What made the change easier was making it clear to us
> that part of using technology is having to take the risk that

what you try at first may not work, or not work as planned. This made it much less threatening to try new things, and the added value was that the kids got to try new things as well. I think that just the continued encouragement and exposure to technology will naturally keep people trying new things, make them comfortable in learning from mistakes. (Personal communication, July 2012)

Another key feature of improvement at Park Manor, and one central to our motion leadership repertoire (see Chapter 3), is that if you want to change something deeply and quickly, *use the group to change the group.* Thus set up the expectation and the means for teachers to continually learn from each other. Several teachers commented on the use of the Sticky Note mentioned earlier: We can see where students are visually; there is consistency across the school; when I see better progress in other classes I can find out why and learn from it; it helps us set school goals; it deepens my understanding of what Level 3 is; I can find out what types of pedagogy can move a student forward.

In an interview with James Bond, he reflected on his own change stance:

You need to be willing to get messy with technology as every tool, program, and application will not work perfectly every time, and tools are always changing.

I tried to make it easy for teachers to use technology by having it in their classrooms set up for them all the time, so they just have to turn it on. I was also willing to help them, so that they would be okay with not knowing how to use it in front of me, and see that it was okay not to use the technology perfectly [debunking the imposter syndrome that we encountered with John Malloy].

As more technology expertise grew in the building, I encouraged the staff to learn from each other and then even from their students. I connected teachers who were learning how to use technology to those teachers who were reluctant to start.

During one staff meeting last February, we toured each classroom, where the teacher shared an application of a technology tool, program, or website, and one piece of evidence of accelerated learning. From this one staff meeting, we were exposed to 16 different examples of how using technology had helped students learn better using the success criteria for accelerated learning.

And during our staff meeting in June, teachers shared one thing they learned from another staff member and its impact on student learning. It was amazing to hear how much learning among staff was going on.

Just as in the best learning with students, you have to create an atmosphere of fun and learning. In *Stratosphere* when I set the first criterion for the new learning as *irresistibly engaging,* I was getting at this element; as was Tony Wagner (2012) when he wrote about "creating innovators," showing that you need to combine "play, passion, and purpose" (p. 26). James states his version as a culture of FIRE (fun, innovation, respect, and excellence). The staff at Park Manor are always sorting out whether a new way or app is value-added or wasteful, including having students be evaluators in this respect.

Another aspect of motion leadership is whether the so-called espoused theory of action by the leader is the one that teachers recognize and can describe and appreciate with equal clarity. Some leaders talk a good game, all the right words are there, but their actions are not authentic or are not experienced as authentic by those with whom they are working. More subtlely, leaders sometimes *think* they are implementing a given practice but may unknowingly be doing so superficially.

If you are a follower, you may perceive the leader's actions as a matter of trust (a leader does not walk the talk) or as lack of clarity (he or she made me an offer I can't understand). So the test is whether the leader and staff experience and appreciate the strategy with equal clarity. Here are a few comments in this regard from a range of teachers at Park Manor:

> James allowed collaboration time with other "informed" staff members—shared apps, sites, and tips with us technologically inept individuals.

> James allowed us to explore technology at our own pace . . . did not push it on us. He encouraged those who were comfortable with new uses and applications to share their successes with us, which in turn made some of us try.

> James helped me ask students how they like to use different technologies and to show me how to use it.

Motion leaders also model what they learn about the change process, including when they made mistakes. James learned from one episode when he veered too much into a push strategy. During one staff meeting, he asked teachers to stand in a circle based on their perceived proficiency with understanding and using technology (those with more knowledge standing in closer). James said he had hoped to show that it doesn't matter where you are in the circle as long as you get a little better and that there is a lot of expertise in the building. What actually happened was that the circle made many staff members self-conscious and embarrassed (both those on the inner and outer circles). James learned that sometimes the best intentions can have negative outcomes.

Lead teacher Liz Anderson says that she found herself sometimes overusing technology. She had to learn that some uses are not best for student learning. She then paid more explicit attention to the links between specific learning activities and accelerated learning. By also focusing on what other staff and students were doing to add value to student learning, she was able to build better integration of technology and learning.

There are many other individual stories among Park Manor staff and students and how the school is expanding its connections—to parents, for example, and to other schools that want to move in similar directions. The bottom line is that Park Manor is on the move with a process that pulls in everyone, uses technology to accelerate learning, gets great results, and generates commitment to do even more.

The six stories in this chapter are different in context but similar in change themes. The skinny of motion leadership is easier than we might have thought, definitely more exciting, and available to any leader and group who are willing to lighten up as they get more serious about the agenda of the moral imperative realized. The essence of motion leadership can be found across the change stories I have been discussing. To condense these lessons, the next chapter lays out the skinny leader's guide to motion leadership. This will be your chance to appreciate the core of motion leadership. When you go on a change journey, you can't afford a lot of baggage. But you need to have a guide—the kind of guide that will fit in your back pocket.

3

THE SKINNY LEADER'S GUIDE TO ACTION

I went to high school at St. Mike's, a Catholic boys' school in Toronto. In those days, there were high-stakes final provincial exams in Grade 13. Many of us taking trigonometry were petrified at the thought of sitting the exam. Fortunately we had a teacher, Fr. Egsgard, who had it figured out. He told us if we mastered a given set of six problems that he presented, we would pass; if we wanted a B mark, we would need to understand a further set; for an A grade he presented a complete set of some 20 types of problems. He had clearly mastered the concept of being on the other side of complexity. He had come through it and knew the skinny of trigonometry. I think I strove to be a B player. I can't remember my mark, but I did pass—much to the amazement of my mother (I didn't tell her about the Egsgard factor).

I had had another priest for Grade 10 history, who shall go nameless. On the last day of school in June, he decided to take a stab at our sex education. Almost as we went out the door to

Father Egsgard, Math Teacher,
St. Mike's High School, Toronto, 1957

start the summer, he had one word of advice for us 16-year-old boys—*abstain* he commanded! Clearly he was operating on the simple side of complexity.

Fr. Egsgard is our skinny leader. He dealt with complex matter but made it understandable and fairly clear in terms of action. Look at his picture. Doesn't he just ooze the demeanor of someone who knows he resides on the right side of complexity?

In this chapter I am going to give you the skinny on motion leadership. There are three tranches to be mastered: A, *the change stance;* B, *the implementation stance;* and C, *the sustainability stance.* If you want to be a good leader, know and become skilled at tranche A; a very good leader will require A + B; and if you want to be a top leader, you will need to know your ABCs in concert; in short, the full-blown motion leader integrates these three stances (Exhibit 3.1).

One other key point: The three stances are not simply linear. You will need to be good at change by paying attention to all three tranches from the beginning. You will need to think of sustainability from day one. You will need to engage in all three on a continuous basis, and so on. Still, you could decide just to be an expert on the change stance, and you would be good (but not great) as a leader.

Exhibit 3.1   The Three Stances of Motion Leadership

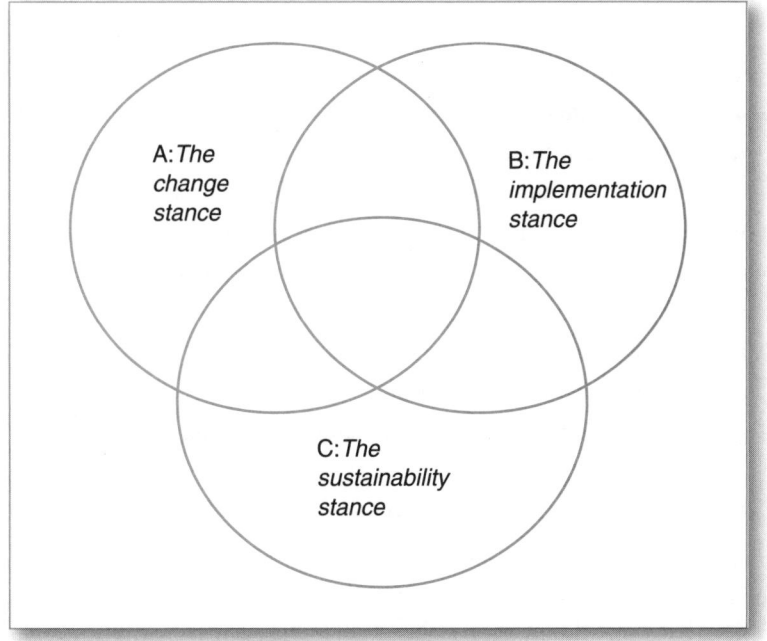

THE CHANGE STANCE

To get us in the change stance mood, let's remember that push-pull-nudge interplay. An example will do nicely. In Ontario we have had some success in increasing high school graduation across the 900 schools, from 68% to 82% in less than 8 years. As we want to keep going, the Learning Secretariat that oversees our strategies came up with the following idea. Someone made the observation that there are an unknown number of students who enter Grade 11 but fail to graduate. How many and who are these people, someone asked. We had the data and calculated that there were more than 14,000 students in question. We then listed the names by school—the 900 schools—and subsequently gave each district the list of names for each high school in its jurisdiction. We also gave districts a small amount of money and said to hire a retired guidance counselor or teacher, find the individuals, and invite them back to school (i.e., make it easy for them to return).

Some 7,000 did return, and of these 2,300 ended up graduating with a high school diploma in June of that year, with many others continuing their program into the subsequent year. I would venture to say that the number who might have returned without any intervention would have been minimal. You see here basically a nudge strategy with a bit of pull.

With this strategy any given change agent can easily slip into a push mode if they are driven by strong moral purpose. One such teacher who was part of a group had taken the district's list of 152 students and had reduced it to 27 students, where they seemed to be stuck. One day the teacher was in the drive-through lane of Tim Horton's donut shop (Timmy's is a Canadian institution with a store every few blocks, it seems). As she reached the pick-up window, she recognized that it was Rick, one of the remaining 27 "lost" students. She said, "Rick, we have been searching all over for you. We want you to come back and talk with us about returning to school on a basis that you might like." He said he wasn't interested, whereupon she said just come in for a chat, no obligation. He said he was sure he didn't want to come back. She then said that she wasn't moving until he agreed to come in for a brief talk. By this time other drivers in line were becoming increasingly impatient. One last attempt by Rick: "Please, miss, move on or I will lose my job." She said, "The answer is no." He finally agreed to come in the following Thursday. Rick did end up returning to school and graduating. The teacher was willing to turn a nudge strategy into a pushy one for a good cause.

In motion leadership we have noticed a paradox about inertia. Most people think that inertia is a powerful resistant force keeping things as they are, which in one sense is true. But if you define inertia as it is meant in physics, you come up with "things like to keep on doing what they're already doing." And then you find that tweaking that direction into a new course is relatively easy in a lot of cases. I recall when I dropped out of university during the first year, finding that I enjoyed playing hockey and hanging around my friends more than I liked going to class. I did not finish the year and took a job at an insurance company. At the time going back to university would never have occurred to me, and because I had left without completing the year or even informing the university that I was leaving, I wouldn't have thought it possible to return.

One day a friend of my father's said out of the blue that he would pay my tuition if I went back to university. For some reason I made an inquiry and was told simply to register again. All it took was one little prompt to get me to inquire, and much to my surprise I was allowed to return. Easy-peasy in retrospect. In the next 8 years I earned my BA, MA, and PhD. I had drifted out and then drifted back into university. My point is that inertia is drift, and not as formidable to alter as we often think.

My colleague Ben Levin (2012b) also reports easy interventions that have high yield, like spending as little as 10 minutes a day talking to a student whom you don't know very well can make a world of difference. In my book *Stratosphere* (Fullan, 2013), I refer to several other research examples that corroborate Ben's observation. In short, the other side of complexity makes you realize that sometimes change can be easier than we thought if we can just get the right leverage and the right timing. This sophistication comes from honing your change stance.

As to the components of the change stance itself, there are seven that I would identify (see Exhibit 3.2). You will find these evident in the motion leaders discussed in Chapter 2.

Exhibit 3.2   Components of the Change Stance

1. Deepen your *moral imperative realized.*
2. *Focus* on a small number of ambitious goals.
3. Build and extend a *guiding coalition.*
4. Toughen your *resolve.*
5. Practice *impressive empathy.*
6. *Push, pull, and nudge.*
7. Think *bigger.*

As we work through these seven elements of the change stance, think of the six vignettes from Chapter 2—Sanger, Hackney, ACT, Hamilton, Uruguay, Park Manor. All were successful (though not quite sure of Uruguay yet), and all had motion leaders who embodied the seven elements in their change stances. As you understand each component think back to the cases, and think of your own experiences that were successful in a big way. My guess is that in successful examples you will see these elements of change at work (this doesn't mean that success is evident at the beginning of the process; by definition the journey is bumpy during the first stages). The goal is to stimulate the motivated, motivate the unmotivated, and, the sweetest of them all, motivate the skeptical and even cynical—and have them thank you at the end of the day. The factors in interaction are where the strength lies. Miss any two or three and your chance stance will be wobbly.

1. Deepen Your Moral Imperative Realized

The moral imperative in education consists of the deep commitment to raising the bar and closing the gap of learning for *all students*. But as they say in Sanger, hope is not a strategy. Lofty vision and mission statements line the drawers and shelves of school districts. This is why we have shifted to the commitment and criterion that you don't really have an imperative unless you are making evidential progress—unless it is going down the road of realization.

We have found that this puts a whole new light on the matter. You begin to think about what would success look like, how do we move the yardsticks, and how do we know we are progressing. When you have this action bias, you appreciate the deeds more than the words. What you find is that when you are getting somewhere, it is a spur to do even more.

At the beginning of this work some 40+ years ago, we assumed the sequence was linear—shared vision, implementation, monitoring, and strengthening. Now the ready-fire-aim metaphor is more apt—ready (moral imperative and initial commitment), fire (learning by purposely doing), and aim (consolidation, drive for more). In many cases the causal action is the reverse of what we might think logically. Instead of commitment causing action, we have action causing commitment. But we are getting ahead of ourselves into implementation; for now the best change start is to establish the realization that realization (accomplishment) is what counts.

Here is where you can start with yourself and your people. Complete the following exercise by answering each of the four questions:

1. What is my moral imperative?
2. How does my moral imperative link to the school and district/system moral imperative?
3. What is the evidence that my moral imperative is being realized?
4. What more could I do to realize my moral imperative in my school *and* in my system?

Now, from the following six quotes (taken from our workshop), circle two that most appeal to you or that you most connect with:

1. The moral imperative needs to be channeled into practice.
2. Effective principals with moral purpose are not successful because they got everyone on board in advance. They got success by building capacity and ownership though cumulative learning.
3. Realization makes teachers soar because they know how to get success, and thus they know it can be done. They become the moral agents of change that drew them into teaching in the first place.
4. District leadership is every bit as essential as school leadership—100% of the schools are implicated.
5. The moral imperative *realized* creates mutual allegiance and collaborative competition. A kind of moral olympics is unleashed.
6. Moral imperative realized is the best working condition a teacher will ever experience.

Now that you have selected your two favorite quotes, complete these two sentences:

I selected this particular quote because . . .

This quote makes me wonder about . . .

This exercise can be done by yourself, with a partner, or with your whole staff. The point is to get the idea of *realization* firmly established at the outset. This is change leaders' most important change stance. They are driven by a moral responsibility to do and accomplish something, and never give up in that quest. In so doing they attract others who become similarly committed. In the end, the crucial point in this section is that moral imperative only has power if you and others are ready to act on it.

This conclusion is reinforced by the findings in the recent comprehensive study of special education inclusion in 10 school districts in Ontario (Hargreaves & Braun, 2012). The researchers did document significant gains in raising the bar and reducing the gap with respect to the academic performance of special education students across the province. Hargreaves and Braun also found that a key document—*Education for All*—was a driving force in the reform because it connected to the "beliefs" of many educators. They observe that beliefs play a big role—prior to change in practice—contrary to the claim by me and others that changes in practice often precede changes in beliefs. Their finding helps us clarify the roles of beliefs and practice.

Hargreaves and Braun's conclusion does in effect confirm that front-end moral imperative is of critical importance. On the matter of beliefs and practices, *both* are crucial. For some, strong new belief documents connect with their values and galvanize them into action. For others, new experiences (practices) lead them to question and change their beliefs. In these cases practice change does lead to belief change. There are still others who may espouse certain beliefs but do not carry them deeply into action; indeed they may not know they are acting superficially. Put another way, just because you say you believe in something doesn't mean that you know what you are doing. The point is that you need to make your moral imperative and your actions a dynamic two-way street. This is the power of moral imperative realized.

2. Focus on a Small Number of Ambitious Goals

The problem is not the absence of goals and improvement effort, but rather the presence of too many innovations that are ad hoc, unconnected, and ever changing. The antidote is to set a small number of ambitious goals, stay with them, and avoid or blunt distracters. In Ontario we have had three big goals and recently added a fourth. The first three consist of raising the bar and closing the gap in literacy, numeracy, and high school graduation. We made sure that these goals were deep (including higher-order skills), across the curriculum (linking the arts and literacy/numeracy), and innovative (new instructional practices, new experiences for students). We recently added early learning—full-day kindergarten for 4- and 5-year-olds, and support and intervention for 0–3-year-olds. We are just beginning down the latter path.

People complain that politics makes it impossible to focus on just a small number of goals, but this is not the case. In addition to trying to influence politicians to focus (with some halting success), we have observed that motion leaders—even if they are on the receiving end, so to speak—carve out a coherent set of goals, small in number. Peter Drucker once observed that entrepreneurs exploit innovation. Motion leaders exploit state policy. Yes, you are stuck with what policymakers do when they generate a range of state policies, but you are not stuck with their mind-sets! The leaders in this book, like Marc

Johnson, faced the same set of constraints as all other districts in the state. Yet they became highly successful. The fact is that under conditions of multiple pressures the change leaders in this book did manage to focus on a small number of ambitious goals, and they had no trouble locating them in the state policy framework.

In short, the commitment to the moral imperative realized will dissipate if it does not have a clear and coherent focus, and if it is not ambitiously and relentlessly pursued. What motion leaders do is to help turn the confusion of ad hoc policies into clarity for those they work with. This is crucial in the current climate. I hope you are beginning to sense momentum as leaders combine change stances 1 and 2.

3. Build and Extend a Guiding Coalition

Right from the get-go, motion leaders know that they can't do it alone. They know that they will need an army of leaders at all levels working in the same direction (but not necessarily agreeing all the time, as we shall see). Although people took Jim Collins's advice to "get the right people on the bus and in the right seats, and get the wrong people off the bus" too literally, this is essentially what happens in building and extending the guiding coalition. The notion is that you need a coherent force of leadership at all levels in order to set the new direction.

At the system level (district or state), you need the lead person who in turn starts to forge a combination of leaders who work together in the same direction. In small districts like Sanger, this means two or three key people to start with; in large systems like Hackney, it means at least a half a dozen leaders. The concept of a guiding coalition was best expressed by our colleague Sir Michael Barber, who gave the hypothetical example of an aggressive newspaper reporter who asks each member of the central team independently a tough question—such as, what is the organization's approach to accountability? Not only would the members of the coalition give consistent responses to the question, they would not even have to think that they would have to check with each other. This is because they interact continually in small and big ways and come to have a similar grasp of the core goals as well as the main strategies that are being employed.

The system then goes about its business by extending the concept to other levels—school principals and teacher leaders, for example. Pretty soon the critical mass of leaders at all levels begins to interact and act in consistent ways, learning from each other and extending the learning to the rest of the organization. It doesn't take long for the system to begin to act in a mutually reinforcing way. The learning is not stagnant because new ideas are being discovered *and processed* on an ongoing basis.

These directions are being reinforced in two ways. First and foremost, in what we call *learning is the work.* The best way of describing this idea is to say that such learning is what happens in between workshops. In essence, this is the day-to-day culture of the organization. We will visit this in the next section, on the implementation stance.

The main point is that no learning intervention is strong enough unless it is inevitably reinforced every day in what comes to be the normal quotidian pattern of organizational life. Admiring the culture of Toyota, Liker and Meier (2007) observe, "If we were to identify the single greatest difference between Toyota and other organizations it would be *the depth of understanding* among Toyota employees regarding their work" (p. 112, emphasis added). Let's say the depth of *shared* understanding. You can't get depth from a workshop. You can't get shared purpose and collective capacity from episodic meetings.

You can get it only from intensive, purposeful interaction and consolidation of what is being learned. You need many leaders, formal and informal, working on this. Examine the six motion leaders in this book in light of the three stances and you will find that they are masters of fostering shared purpose through action.

Second, these directions must be reinforced through personnel or human resource policies. (By contrast, you can't cause culture change by just using personnel policies as the driver; in our language culture is the driver and personnel is the reinforcer.) Thus, job descriptions (of school leaders, for example), criteria for promotion, mentoring, and performance appraisal are all used to strengthen the presence of leaders working together.

One example we saw from Hackney was when the chair of the Learning Trust said that headteachers are expected to work for the common good of the authority as a whole by helping each other achieve goals. This expectation was then backed up by leaders monitoring and providing feedback on performance, including dismissal of those (few) who did not move in the desired direction. Another example we know of is Jamie McCracken, when he was director of Ottawa Catholic District School Board. The system was clearly building a new collaborative culture when Jamie met with the 85 or so vice principals at his annual get-together with them. At that meeting Jamie stated in no uncertain terms,

> If you want to get promoted in this system from where you
> are, you will need to have a track record in instructional
> leadership. We will provide you with many opportunities
> to acquire the skills, but if you do not avail yourselves of
> these, don't bother applying for promotion.

How's that for a pushy stance to build consistent school leadership?

Focus on building and extending a guiding coalition through learning as the work is backed up by human resource policies, and pretty soon you have a critical mass that only gets stronger year after year.

4. Toughen Your Resolve

It is at about this stage that you will need to strengthen your resolve. In the early stages of any new direction, it is tough slugging. As Machiavelli (1532/2007) observed 500 years ago, there is nothing more difficult to handle than to initiate a new order of things: "For the reformer has enemies in all those who profit by the old order; and only lukewarm defenders in all those who would profit by the new order" (p. 19).

This situation is alleviated by the guiding coalition (i.e., there are increasingly more people on board, but still it is tough slugging). Perhaps the most difficult psychological problem is that you, as a leader, are putting in long hours, driven by the moral imperative, but people are complaining. Put another way, you are working your guts out for the organization and the good of others, but you are not being appreciated. People with the combination of moral imperative and tough resolve can handle not being popular at this stage of the change process.

Motion leaders need to have the capacity to keep going even when they are receiving little praise. This needs to be recognized as normal, as par for the course at the beginning of a new change process. In a phrase, don't expect many compliments early in the change process. This is why leaders need resilience, persistence, ability to change tacks without going off course, and an all-around capacity to stay the course without being rigid, but above all without giving up. In short, they persist but are alert to feedback.

These characteristics are identified in the Ontario Leadership Framework (OLF) (Institute for Educational Leadership, 2012) prepared by my close colleague Ken Leithwood. The OLF notes that complex jobs have more than their share of ambiguity, risk, and uncertainty. Leaders operating under these conditions need certain psychological resources beyond the ordinary. The OLF research identifies three in particular: optimism, self-efficacy, and resilience. Exactly!

Motion leaders have confidence (a sense of self-efficacy); positive expectations about succeeding now and in the future (optimism); and perseverance toward goals, including redirecting paths to goals and the capacity to bounce back when beset by problems and adversity (resilience). This OLF research is based on considerable evidence and is congruent with our own cases of success. One's confidence is strengthened perhaps by the inner feeling that one is gaining on the problem or soon will.

But there is one more early hurdle; How do you handle, and equally important avoid, mishandling resistance?

5. Practice Impressive Empathy

We all know what empathy is, but what is "impressive empathy"? It is having empathy for someone who is in your way. That's why it is impressive! You wish they would get out of the way or go away. And remember that having empathy for someone else does not mean that you agree with them, but rather that you understand them as if you were in their shoes. Especially at the early stages, you need to relate to people in terms of where they are coming from. *Being right is not a strategy.* You have to build relationships, including with many who may be against the new direction.

A corollary of this change stance is the need to give respect before the other party has deserves it or earned it. I learned this by watching how leaders acted in toxic situations in order to get positive movement. I think of Ryan Friedman of Crosby Heights Elementary School in York Region, just north of Toronto. He became principal of a school that had such a pervasive negative culture. The highest number of management grievances of any school in the district, parents wanting to move their kids, low morale for all, dilapidated building—you name it.

Ryan is a respectful leader who also has most of the other qualities of our change stance. Do you think in that first month as he acted with utmost respect for everyone that he got much respect back? Not a chance! People had learned to be disrespectful, and it is unlikely if not impossible that they would reciprocate when at first they were treated differently. Ryan persisted, added capacity building, focused on the moral imperative realized, and within 3 years the six official test results (reading, writing, and math for each of Grades 3 and 6) doubled from an average of 42% to 84%.

You can be demanding—tough without losing your tenderness, as Miguel Brechner put it—but if you do not bring a positive stance to a difficult situation, you have no chance of changing it for the better.

Remember, these core elements interact. By this time you have an increasing number of things going for you. Now your sophistication as a change leader is really on the line. You need to think about how you approach change itself. This is the real skinny of change savvy because you have to sort through how and when to use push, pull, and nudge, realizing that all three will be needed. But how do you keep them in balance in order to get maximum movement forward?

6. Push, Pull, and Nudge

Andy Hargreaves and I worked out many of the ideas on push, pull, and nudge with school leaders and teams in our workshop tour in the UK in June 2012. I can't tell you the exact combination of push, pull, and nudge that you will need to use because each situation calls for different timing, but I can tell you that you will be well served as a change leader by employing this repertoire. You always need all three in action. The chemistry varies according to the situation. Let's start with the easiest of the three—nudge. As I said, Thaler and Sunstein (2008) note that people are "nudge-able"; we don't always have to use overt change strategies.

Make the new things accessible without requiring people to do anything. For example, putting fresh fruit at the end of a cafeteria line (instead of potato chips and chocolate bars) can result in new choices for some people. In educational change the biggest nudge factor, I think, is transparency of data and practice. Just as if you automatically received your weight the moment your feet hit the ground every morning, mere transparency can make a difference. With nudge, you don't have to do anything beyond making it very easy for people to encounter and access whatever the new practices are. As a change agent you need to arrange such possibilities, but you don't need to fret over the uptake. So always use the nudge factor, and be pleasantly surprised.

In addition, we need to be more proactive, and here is where the dilemma of push-and-pull comes into play. Push involves strategies that require people to do certain things, or demands that they do so, or makes the expectations explicit that they should do so. Policies that require teachers to work together in this school for the good of the kids and principals to be instructional leaders are two such examples. The trouble of course is that you can't always *make* people act in new ways. And you can never make them act newly if they are not capable of doing so. But if you have strong moral purpose and a sense of urgency, you do want to get pushy for the sake of the kids. What makes the change stance effective is that motion leaders put into place the processes and structures that pull and push people in new directions. They know that creating a new normal is more effective than issuing orders.

Pull strategies *attract* people to the new thing—a compelling vision, a chance for adventure, an opportunity to develop and grow with colleagues, or a process of engagement that promises to make a difference in the lives of students is compelling for some. My friend Andy Hargreaves likes to say, "Pull if you can, and push if you must," because he thinks those in authority resort to the push lever too readily (and in any case it doesn't work to get the new behavior). I mainly agree, but I also take the position that sometimes you need to be pushy.

In our moral imperative realized work, we have often required people to participate (albeit it nonjudgmentally on our part during the process) and later heard from reluctant ones that they ended up gaining substantially from the experience. Motivate the unmotivated and have them thank you for it later. I think of a veteran Grade 4 teacher who reluctantly entered a series of coaching sessions, got great new responses from her students, and was rejuvenated. Sometimes people don't know what they don't know.

Thus we cannot say in the abstract whether to use push or pull strategies, but we can say that *elements of both* should always be present, with one or the other having the upper hand for some individuals or in some situations. When you think of Hackney, the push that all kids should learn was always in your face, but so was the help and camaraderie of working together and getting results whereby people were drawn in (pulled) to do more and more.

There are some other refinements. Most of us have a tendency to be stronger on one or the other trait (push or pull). You need, then, to look at yourself—or even better, get feedback so that you can build up your weaker side. Leaders who are all push better reassess. Those who are all pull better worry about whether they are getting enough buy-in. Work on your weakness while appreciating your strength.

Another wise step is to complement your qualities by adding someone to the team who has different traits. If you are all push, hire a pull deputy (but don't try to push him or her around). If you are too pully, hire a more demanding second in command and openly discuss and assess what works for you and your organization.

You will see that virtually all of the other motion leadership traits across the three stances use push-and-pull strategies. The idea is to figure out what works in your situation at this particular time and to be sensitive to the combination of push, pull, and nudge that gets best results. As a general rule I would say that you have to be more pushy than pully at the beginning of a change process, and the reverse—rely more on pull—once you are getting some success. As we will see, once you have built some capacity you can rely on or use the group to keep going. Indeed, a group that has a lot of high capacity members can effectively integrate push and pull to go deeper.

In the final analysis, however, it is an empirical question—be aware of your push-pull-nudge tendencies and determine what is actually working. In other words, learn from what actions are "moving" the organization forward. Motion leaders are always learning.

7. Think Bigger

We have been increasingly working on what we call whole-system reform because we concluded that piecemeal or small-scale reform will never add up. In order to change the whole system, we will need two things: system leaders who commit to policies and strategies that focus on the system as a whole and, perhaps even more important, a myriad of change leaders at all levels who are engaged in changing bigger chunks of the system.

The advice to the motion leader is that whatever you are working on, try enlarging your scope by at least one notch. This is what led Marc Johnson of Sanger and the other seven superintendents in California to form the CORE group that I described in Chapter 1. Most of them had been very successful in their own districts. Not even sustainability in their districts was sufficient for the next stage (although it was deeply important). They wanted (as a natural extension, I would say) to contribute to the betterment of other districts and regions by doing whatever they could to help make the California school system more effective. In short, as they experienced success in one situation, they naturally wanted to make a bigger contribution. This is a basic human tendency for leaders who are committed to moral imperative realized.

More generally, *think bigger* means that the classroom teacher wants to work on improving the school as a whole, the principal wants to work with other principals to enable every school in the district to become better, district superintendents want the state to improve, and so on. As I interact more and more with what I call the PISA crowd (the 70 or so nations that participate in the Organisation for Economic Co-operation and Development's Programme for International Student Assessment), I find more and more state leaders interested not only in learning from other countries but also in contributing what they know to others. Even in a selfish sense, educated countries make for better neighbors. Thus, motion leaders are big thinkers and big doers!

This pretty much brings us to implementation. Of course change knowledge is essential through all three stances, so carry forward the seven elements of change as you go from here. I also said, with the help of Fr. Egsgard, that you can stop reading right here if you are content with being a *good change agent*. You can do a hell of a lot of good by honing the seven skill sets of the change stance. There is nothing at all wrong with that. The world would be a much better place if we had leaders who evinced these seven change qualities we just covered.

But if you want to go from good to very good, you need to become obsessed with implementation.

THE IMPLEMENTATION STANCE

Implementation has been my bread and butter since my rookie days around 1970. John Goodlad had discovered that looking behind the classroom door was a different world. He and his fellow researchers found not only that innovations that were claimed to be in use were not evident, but also that innovations that people did not acknowledge that they were engaged in were sometimes observed in their very classrooms. Seymour Sarason had concluded loud and clear that the more things change, the more they remain the same. The development of big, high-profile curriculum innovations in math, science, and social studies that flourished during the 1960s came a cropper on the rocks of implementation once we observed what was actually (not) happening.

Implementation—the quality of what is put into practice—became the sine qua non of change. It has now taken its place in the whole-system arena. We are no longer thinking of just implementing this or that curriculum but also wanting to change the entire culture of the system and its organizational subparts; hence the implementation stance (see Exhibit 3.3).

Exhibit 3.3   The Implementation Stance

1. *Premature excitement* is fragile.
2. Make *capacity building* central.
3. Beware of *fat plans.*
4. *Communication during implementation* is paramount.
5. Have *purposeful data permeate.*
6. *Use the group to change the group.*

Let's start with a primer on strategy. Strangely, most strategy documents do not focus on implementation. Richard Rumelt (2011) tells us that there is a big difference between good and bad strategy, and it is not apparent on paper. He says simply being ambitious is not a strategy. Most often he finds that plans contain high-sounding goals but no coherent strategy to get there. Bad strategies tend to skip over pesky details such as problems.

Essentially a good strategy diagnoses the situation, anticipates problems, prepares for taking action, and realizes the likelihood that surprises will be encountered. Bad strategies contain highfalutin words, fail to acknowledge probable challenges, and mistake goals for strategy. They are "long on goals and short on action" (p. 36). Playing right into skinny hands, Rumelt notes that "a hallmark of true expertise and insight is making a complex subject understandable. A hallmark of mediocrity and bad strategy is unnecessary complexity—a flurry of fluff masking an absence of substance" (p. 40). To paraphrase Nietzsche, when leaders don't know what they are doing, they often muddy the waters in order to make them seem deep. Motion leaders understand current reality so that they can find the levers to new, better realities. The next time you see a strategic plan, ask yourself: Does it contain real actions in relation to causing positive movement forward? The six elements of the implementation stance are realistically connected to action and improvement therein.

1. Premature Excitement Is Fragile

"Guess who has been at the latest workshop" is a familiar refrain by the back-home folks when the leader or a leadership team comes back from an exciting professional learning event. Lone or small teams of innovators have heaps of excitement and energy, but not only do they not inspire others when they return for action, *they annoy them*. In our ready-fire-aim metaphor, leaders do not get bogged down at the front-end stage, getting in a froth about ambitious futures—even moral imperative ones. They should be enthusiastic but realize that the hard step is commencing a process whereby others get excited. They define the task as generating positive contagion, including among the skeptics.

The change stance we discussed earlier helps because it confronts real problems. If excitement is greater than fulfillment, it is because actual fulfillment rarely follows hyped-up excitement. Implementation buffs are wary of front-end frenzy, preferring instead to create the real McCoy of accomplishment. It may be early success but it is nonetheless real. Motion leaders know that actual success has a sticky quality because it is emotionally grabbing, because it represents skill development at work, and because it shows people that it can be done.

So don't eliminate your pre-action enthusiasm, but create and look for the early wins of real implementation—improved quality of practice. Make actual success the basis of excitement.

2. Make Capacity Building Central

Of all of our strategies, the one that has the greatest power is developing new capacities in individuals and groups. I tend to put these competencies into two bins. One concerns instructional or pedagogical capabilities tuned to learning for all students; the other refers to *change knowledge* (i.e., the change stance)—the capacity to motivate the unmotivated and to create powerful collaboration. If you are a would-be motion leader, you better not stop at the notion that teachers should have capacity to do this or that. And if they don't have enough of the capacity that you think is needed, you also better not confine yourself to the individualistic strategy that you can just hire for it, or appraise your way into it by individual rewards and punishments. If you want to get somewhere quickly, make your core strategy capacity building applied to the setting in which you work.

This has certainly been the case in our Ontario strategy. Focus the new work on a small number of ambitious goals, and create many opportunities to make the capacities essential for accomplishing them part and parcel of *learning is the work*. Establish personnel policies that reinforce the direction you are moving. Make the main role of leaders at all levels a capacity-building proposition.

It is amazing how much you can move a system, even a large one, within 3 years with this strategy. This is because you are developing the skills and the ownership essential for success. And once many people are engaged, they rub off on each other in a positive way and send powerful messages to those not getting on board. Skills, clarity, and ownership lead to progress, and the latter generates pride and motivation to do more.

Capacity building is not just workshops and courses. It is always what happens in between workshops that count. Day-to-day culture is central to the capacity-building agenda.

3. Beware of Fat Plans

Using skinny language, the problem of fat plans was in my first book on Motion Leadership. The issue has become much more clear now, and since the problem persists we give it an encore for this addition. Rumelt (2011) calls bad strategic plans (our fat plans) "a dog's breakfast of objectives" (p. 53). He cites as an example a strategic plan from the mayor's office in a Pacific Northwest city that contained 47 strategies and 178 action items. Action item number 122 was "to create a strategic plan"!

We could cite 100 other examples, but let's take one of ours. A director of one of the school districts in Ontario called me and said, "We are using all your strategies and we are getting bogged down. People are getting frustrated and are ready to give up. Would you come and take a look," he requested. I asked him to send me the district improvement plan. It was 31 pages long, contained 16 goals, and had eight headings across the top of the matrix that indicated resources, evaluation, timelines, and the like. Not as bad as the mayor's strategic plan, but still a fat plan that wouldn't move much.

I asked the director to reduce the goals to three big ones and said that we would come do a few sessions with their school teams (all 41 of them). They had no trouble centering on three core goals. We did a series of six sessions with them. Having been stuck for 4 years, they moved ahead in most student achievement measures by an average of 8% the following year. When we observed the school teams present their work to each other, they clearly knew what they were doing. There was excitement, pride, and enthusiasm—they couldn't wait to do more.

The best rendition of the problem of plans comes from Doug Reeves (2009), who found that "the size and the prettiness of the implementation plan are inversely related to the quality of action and the impact on student learning" (p. 81). The greater and more elaborate the plan looks on paper, the *less* impressive it is in action. The implementation plan is actually not for the planners (even though that is how it often works psychologically). Plans should be *for the implementers!* Now the solution becomes obvious. Plans have to relate to the world of implementers—they must be clear, actionable, inspiring—in a word, they must be "sticky." They must be skinny and punch above their weight.

Another refinement has become clear since the problem of fat plans first surfaced. State and federal governments require elaborate plans in order to grant approval and/or money. Even though such exercises are by and large a waste of resources, I accept these bureaucratic realities. No problem. Send the fat plans upward to get the money and the skinny plans downward to get the action.

Be true to day-to-day implementation and you shall be rewarded.

4. Communication During Implementation Is Paramount

The positioning of communication is another one of our carry-overs that continues to be edifying. In our workshops we show a video of a CEO of a borough who was hired to develop a new vision and strategy for the municipality. The person is articulate, engaging, and exudes trustworthiness. She spent a whole year talking around the place with countless sessions giving and seeking input. When a survey was conducted to see what people thought of the new vision that emerged, she found that 80% had never heard that there was a vision, and of the remainder only 20% were in favor. In other words, huge expenditure of energy resulted in a puny 4% in favor of the new vision (20% of 20%).

How could that be? Again, knowledge of implementation tells us that talk in the absence of action is *almost meaningless.* Not fully but mostly meaningless because it is not grounded. It is action that generates questions, furnishes clarity if well handled, develops skills, and leads to ownerships if accompanied by good implementation processes. We are right back to Rumelt—coherent action and embedded problem solving serve two purposes. They provide many opportunities to clarify and refine the vision tied to action, and they enable leaders and implementers to address the problems of implementation that are being experienced.

As a leader, commit yourself to facing the reality of implementation. Make it clear that change is a two-way partnership, that you are on a purposeful learning journey together, that you will be seeking many opportunities to find out how well it is going (what is working) and what might be problematic (in response to which you will problem-solve). We know that a climate of nonjudgmentalism—learning from mistakes—is essential. Implementation, especially at the beginning of a change process, can never be smooth. If you don't make it clear at the outset that implementation is a learning journey, you will be dead in the water.

Pre-implementation communication is important, but don't rely on it to carry more freight than it can manage. Save your energy for use where it will really counts—during implementation.

5. Have Purposeful Data Permeate

> *Statistics are a wonderful servant and an appalling master.*
>
> *Hopper and Hopper (2007, p. 125)*

The role of data in the change process presents one of the trickiest implementation problems. But its good side is that data can be a trifecta winner: Mere openness of results and practice can nudge people to pay attention to progress. Data are hard to avoid when they are ever present. Second, they can push people to act when others are moving forward and you are stagnant even when no one comments on the situation. And third, they can be powerful pullers when you are getting somewhere and can't wait to do more, or when your colleagues are becoming successful and you seek to understand why.

The most important thing for motion leaders to know about data is that you need to position the use of data primarily as a *strategy for improvement* and let public accountability be a derivative. This indirect approach requires discipline. Many systems have tried to use data as a direct force for accountability only to see it backfire. This, what I call the "wrong driver," can never work on any scale because people are not motivated by external accountability. Instead you need to use data as central to improvement of practice and position accountability accordingly. You will in fact get better public accountability in this manner.

On the negative side, schools systems are flooded with data that are too voluminous, untimely, imprecise, and not linked to action. In every case of success, we see assessment data and instructional practice working in tandem. Lyn Sharratt and I call it "putting the FACES on data" (Sharratt & Fullan, 2012). It is personalization (to the student by name and by face), and it is for each and every student—100%. In Park Manor, with their Sticky Notes on where each student stands, the principal and teachers can tell you on any given day where every student is in reading, writing, and math performance; what their strengths and weaknesses are; and what strategies will be necessary to move forward.

This attention to detail is key. Pick a student's name out of a hat, and the principal can tell you within 10 minutes how well that student is doing as of that particular day. It is this precision and responsive action that enables a school to double its performance from, say, 40% proficiency to 80% or more. These leaders make it clear that data are used primarily for improvement. They don't judge the results as much as they say, "Okay, where are we and what are you—and we—going to do to get even better?" This stance gets people focusing on improvement.

Of course, these leaders don't ignore accountability. They just know that it arises from internal commitment to performance. This so-called internal accountability is a function of good data, associated improvement actions, transparency for all (including parents), and all the other factors identified in the three stances laid out in this chapter. In every case this constellation of factors results in stronger public accountability because it almost always produces results and everything is in the open. Tough decisions are made along the way, but they occur within a climate of improvement.

Once again, even if the larger system has a punitive approach to accountability, motion leaders realize that while they may be stuck with the policy, they are not stuck with the mind-set. They can literally redefine the meaning of how data are primarily used. Regardless of what the center does, you can use data constructively for school improvement at the local level.

As a motion leader you must come to the table with solid data.

6. Use the Group to Change the Group

The most powerful force for implementation is how the group behaves. We know this intuitively. The group can be powerfully negative (e.g., gangs, sexist corporate cultures) or powerfully positive (e.g., when close-knit team members go to the wall for each other). In education, let's take a simple, straightforward example. Carrie Leana, a business professor at the University of Pittsburgh, conducted an elegant piece of research in 135 elementary schools in New York City. She measured only three things: human capital (the individual paper qualifications of teachers), social capital (how teachers responded to the question: Do teachers in this school work together in a trusted purposeful way to improve student learning and achievement?), and math results (at the beginning and end of the year).

You can see where I am heading. Leana found that schools with high social capital outperformed (increased math scores) schools with high human capital. Those with both high human capital and high social capital did best. She also found that teachers with low human capital who worked in a high social capital environment improved more in the course of a year than their low human capital counterparts who worked in schools with lower social capital. The group, in other words, rubs off on you in positive ways if they are busy doing good things together.

If you ask yourself what is easier, going from human to social capital or the reverse, the answer is pretty obvious. No matter how good you are as an individual, chances are you will be picked off by a negative culture. Yes, outstanding individual principals can turn around a toxic culture, but it is a hell of an uphill battle. Consequently, there are a dearth of leaders who can do this. Consider the reverse: A teacher with low human capital goes into a school with high social capital. It will be very hard for that teacher to stay in the school and not improve.

In short, if you want to get deep change within reasonable time periods, you need strategies that are based on developing social capital. The role of leadership is to build collaborative cultures in schools; to establish clusters of schools that learn from each other in a purposeful, focused manner; to change the culture of the district, not just the schools; and to foster a sense of systemness in the state, province, and country. Systemness is appreciation of the big picture and a commitment to contributing to the success of the state. To be successful in this, you need the group.

Finally, it is not just getting groups together and letting them loose. This is a disciplined operation. The best way to think about it is to realize that effective group work is reinforced by the seven change stance qualities and the first five implementation stance factors that we just discussed. If these twelve elements are in line, then the group will be a powerful additive to getting substantial, lasting change.

In sum, the six components of the implementation stance place you at the scene of the action, where you should be as a leader. Recall the finding from the research on the role of the school principal in impacting schoolwide student learning. Vivianne Robinson found five factors that were important, but one stood out twice as important as any other—the degree to which the principal *participates as a learner* in working with staff to move the school forward. As a first-year principal you would not necessarily be very good at this, but do it for 5 years and you will have learned a lot. There is no substitute for being there, which is why obsession with implementation is so critical.

Now you have two stances going for you: change and implementation. If you become adept in both domains, you will have gone from adequate to good to very good as a change leader. You could make a whole career of these two stances and retire quite peacefully. But perhaps you might want to leave a lasting legacy. Sustainability is your final responsibility: how to make a contribution after you are gone!

THE SUSTAINABILITY STANCE

Sustainability has inertia going for it. If you can just get many of the right things in motion, and reinforce them while you are there, you increase the chances of things continuing after you have gone. There are three things you need to get in place (see Exhibit 3.4).

Exhibit 3.4   The Sustainability Stance

1. Stay the course.
2. Leadership for all—position leadership for the present and the future.
3. Balance improvement and innovation.

1. Stay the Course

We already have *toughen your resolve* as the fourth change quality because there are many obstacles at the beginning of the process and one can easily give up too soon. Once there has been some implementation success, it is also easy to get complacent. Some of the persistence required at this stage will be about content priorities. There is always more work to do on literacy, numeracy, and high school graduation to continue to raise the bar and close the gap. The process and culture will need attention—continuous investment in capacity building; databases and usage; push, pull, and nudge; and, of course, thinking and going bigger will never be done.

There will and should be new things, but not directions that neglect and undo the careful work that has been accomplished. Many successful leaders lose interest after several years of focusing on certain initiatives. This tendency can be combated by combining two stances. First realize that continuity of direction is one of your crucial forward responsibilities. Second and simultaneously, pursue new ideas—innovations and developments—that might represent next effective practices. This is tricky, but motion leaders know that sustaining and improving current priorities while exploring promising new ones is not mutually exclusive. In short, cultivate the dynamic relationship between continuing and new practice (see point 3).

2. Leadership for All—Position Leadership for the Present and the Future

The extension of leadership will have been a priority since day one, when the guiding coalition was first formed. The purpose of the guiding coalition was to provide focus and consistency and begin the process of fostering leaders everywhere. One you think about whole-system reform, you will know that you need leaders at all levels—school, district, and state. In one very real way, you are developing leaders who have the change, implementation, and sustainability stances we are describing here. Mentors upon mentors, peers learning leadership from each other, mutual allegiances and collaborative competition, and so on.

Collaborative leadership makes two fundamental contributions. First, you get more done in the short run when many leaders are working on the same agenda. In fact, the job is too big if there are not scores of leaders working together on the same priorities. For sustainability there is a bonus. If you are really always developing collaborative leadership, it means that the junior members are being groomed as the next generation of leaders. When we think of the school principalship, we say that your job is twofold: to focus relentlessly on the student achievement agenda and to deliberately develop leadership in others as you do this. Put one way, the main mark of effective leaders when they retire is not just how much impact they have had on student performance, but also how many good leaders they leave behind. Usually it is not turnover of leaders that is the big problem in success stories, but rather *discontinuity of direction.*

From the day you start, you need to plan to leave a legacy—and that legacy is leadership strength in others. This may be your most important gift to the organization.

3. Balance Improvement and Innovation

Improvement is increasing the efficacy of current practice; innovation is developing new ideas that would be a departure from existing practice that might have greater promise. As I said, it is necessary to think of continuous improvement of existing practice while you consider what might be next. This means that improvement will be more obvious because you are working with refinements of what you are already doing. Innovation, at the early stages, will be more exploratory. In lean startup language, the newer things at first will appear as *minimal viable products* (see my discussion in *Stratosphere* [Fullan, 2013]). Thus their longer term potential will require further development. I don't think I can place a precise value on the balance of improvement and innovation, but I can say that you need to engage in both.

The distinction between improvement and innovation is receiving wider attention and is beyond the scope of this book to delve into in detail. Hargreaves and Shirley (2012), in their book *The Global Fourth Way*, devote an entire chapter on "the paradox of innovation and improvement." Michael Barber and his colleagues (2012) dive into "Oceans of Innovations" and conclude that we have to engage in "whole-system reform" (continuing improvements of entire systems) while we cultivate "systemic innovations." Several of us are currently exploring how these two "systems" can co-exist and feed on each other.

This is not just an academic pursuit. It is indeed the situation we now face in Ontario. First, some improvements may be best thought of as extensions and improvements of what you are already doing. After 8 years of pretty successful reforms, we want to go even deeper on the existing agenda to raise the bar and close the gap relative to literacy and numeracy across the curriculum.

We also need to look to the future in new proactive ways. Current education systems—even the front-runners—have pretty much reacher their peak of performance. Radical innovation is required to reach new heights of learning that are deeply engaging for students and teachers. In *Stratosphere,* I predict that we will soon be at a tipping point for establishing a new learning partnership between students and teachers that will be greatly accelerated by technology (provided that pedagogy is the driver). Currently, students are bored as they move up the grades, and teachers are increasingly alienated because, for a variety of reasons, they are not able to break through and reach students at a deeper level.

The innovation that I see here (and indeed we are working on one such example in our Madcap Learning Systems) will require a new learning partnership between students and teachers. This new pedagogy will have students individually and in small groups more in charge of their own learning and will have teachers as change agents—activators and monitors of learning processes and outcomes. We can see glimpses already of what this looks like, but only that—minimal viable products, if you like.

The new pedagogical learning partnership between and among students and teachers will demand a deep transformation in the nature of how learning occurs. We are, excitingly so, entering unknown territory. When John Hattie (2012) found in his metastudies that "teachers as facilitators" generates only 0.17 effect sizes on student learning, while "teachers as activators" has a 0.60 impact, he opened up a whole new world of questions. We now have our work cut out to discover what this new pedagogical partnership looks like in practice and how to achieve it on a systemwide scale.

Thus radical new ideas are afoot with huge transformational potential. My prediction is that this will be a rich and rapidly expanding area in the immediate future. Change leaders, then, will need to continue improvements while they examine the new learning scenarios that integrate the powers of technology, new pedagogy, and change knowledge—the latter containing the very motion leadership stances we are talking about in this chapter. The skinny leader's guide to action has never been so essential as it is now.

In short, sustainability means both "maintainability" (improvement) and "adaptability" (innovation) to changes in the environment that demand new innovative responses (my thanks to Andy Hargreaves for pointing this out). With the three stances internalized you are in a better position to contend with these complex challenges. We can't unravel all the issues you will face as you go from setting to setting, but we can say that the skills of motion leadership and the three stances therein will serve you well in this journey.

So there you have it, the Skinny Leader's Guide to Motion Leadership (see Exhibit 3.5). Not too much to remember: three stances and 16 qualities therein. Many of them synergize so that you learn several simultaneously. You practice them, hopefully with good mentors, and you get even better. Take action, use the change stances as a checklist, and realize that you are constantly honing your skinny skills of motion leadership.

Exhibit 3.5   The Skinny Leader's Guide to Motion Leadership

Stance	Components
The Change Stance	1. Deepen your *moral imperative realized*. 2. *Focus* on a small number of ambitious goals. 3. Build and extend a *guiding coalition*. 4. Toughen your *resolve*. 5. Practice *impressive empathy*. 6. *Push, pull, and nudge*. 7. Think *bigger*.
The Implementation Stance	1. *Premature excitement* is fragile. 2. Make *capacity building* central. 3. Beware of *fat plans*. 4. *Communication during implementation* is paramount. 5. Have *purposeful data permeate*. 6. *Use the group to change the group*.
The Sustainability Stance	1. Stay the course. 2. Leadership for all—position leadership for the present and the future. 3. Balance improvement and innovation.

Still, checklists are checklists and there is nothing like the real McCoy. For the latter we need to return to our flesh-and-blood motion leaders. The ones, by name and situation, we started with in Chapter 1. They learned a lot in getting successes in one setting, especially impressive because they helped cause whole-system reform in most cases. But what is it like to move on to a new challenge? How well does motion leadership savvy travel? We will take a peek at what's next for some of these leaders.

4

WHAT'S NEXT

W e don't know what will be next for New York City. After 10 years using mostly wrong drivers that took a negative toll on the hearts and minds of many educators, there is a group that wants to alter the course and go for whole-system reform with different strategies, more in line with motion leadership principles. It would be impressive to see 1,600 schools on the move under very challenging circumstances. We should look for ideas that emerge for the next phase of reform in New York and see to what extent the new strategies encompass motion leadership principles.

It is also too early to tell how Uruguay has been faring with its curious strategy of comprehensive technology "without complicating the lives of teachers." We will be able to report on our findings next year. We will see what happens when pull is fortified with more push. I should say that unlike the other cases in earlier chapters we do not know whether Uruguay will be a success. At this stage it is a curiosity.

We wish Hamilton-Wentworth District School Board well, and expect that it will build on its initial success in taking a bureaucratic system and loosening it up for new purposes. It is revealing to note that tighter bureaucracies generate weaker focus than less structured but more normatively committed groups of educators. Coherence is generated through more focused cultures because they produce new *shared mind-sets,* not just aligned structures. Coherence on the ground is always more powerful than structural alignment on paper.

Park Manor will no doubt continue to go deeper, but will it remain a one-school phenomenon? As Shania Twain would say if it stays as a single school, "That don't impress me much." We need whole-system reform.

We can take a closer look in this chapter at three cases entering new phases. What will Marc Johnson do now that he is entering the end of a successful tenure at Sanger Unified School District? What about Trish Okoruwa at Hackney, now that she is in charge and faces a whole new governance arrangement? And Jim Watterston going from ACT to Victoria—a much larger system with a decade of doing many of the right things and not much to show for it?

In each of these cases we will examine the lessons that these leaders say they learned in their previous successful stints, and then we will ask them what their plans are for the new challenge. We can't predict that their new systems will improve in the next couple of years or more, but it will be instructive to consider how previously successful leaders approach new, specific circumstances.

Once more I should say that I use these leaders by name to personify motion leadership. Each of them would stress that any success comes from many leaders and others who worked with them. Keep in mind that they did not do this alone. Indeed, their success is due to the widespread leadership that occurred as part and parcel of the strategies that they and their colleagues employed.

It will be interesting to see how the accounts of the three leaders align with the 16 motion leader qualities that I identified in Chapter 3. I formulated these characteristics prior to receiving the reflections from the three leaders. Of course, I knew them and had worked with them, so one could expect that I would know their main approaches, but it is one thing to think you know what they would say, and another to see what they *actually say* in explaining what strategies they are using. When leaders readily describe what they are doing, with what success, and what they are learning, you can be pretty sure that they are good motion leaders. Effective leaders walk the talk, but they are very clear when they explain what they are doing and why (they talk the walk in precise ways). Let's see how their accounts measure up against the 16 qualities.

So from the horses' mouths, what change lessons have been learned and what might be next? What do California, Australia, and Hackney have to tell us about lessons for success, and how one would take them forward to new situations?

SANGER

The material in this section comes directly from Marc Johnson and from a third-party evaluation of the performance of the district. We know the objective results; in motion leadership, we are also interested in what is going on in the heads of the leaders as they get results, reflect on lessons learned, and contemplate what might be next.

The first observation that Marc has is that there is no ceiling to improvement. It is not "How good do we have to be?" but rather "How good can we be?" To use a sports analogy, there is always another record to be broken. One also sees a common thread through these success stories: A key to constant improvement is to always work on increased capacity, especially the capacity of leaders at all levels. Leaders developing other leaders relative to a focused agenda is the central driver. Marc also has accountability well placed. It is a matter of "reciprocal accountability," he stresses, which means that if I as leader have an expectation for anyone in the organization, I also have an obligation to build the capacity of that individual to help meet that expectation.

The deep goal at Sanger was to change the culture and to avoid quick program fixes. We saw in Chapter 2 some of the ways in which Sanger has accomplished this goal, but now the question is: As the two top leaders are about to leave, how deep is the culture? The external evaluators confirm that Sanger has created a solid dynamic system, which is evident in the ways that they do the following:

- solicit feedback formally and informally
- create multiple intersecting learning communities, which build relationships not only among peers within schools, but also across schools and between schools and the district office
- monitor data frequently
- adapt to changes by identifying and solving problems as they arise
- constantly adjust what is tight and what is loose in response to feedback, balancing central direction with autonomy
- seek new information by networking outside the district

These elements form the glue of focus and coherence among Sanger educators. If we take the more formal conclusions of the external evaluation, we begin to see confirmation of many of the 16 elements of our change leader stances.

Sanger's success came from a systemwide endeavor that included these principles:

1. Think big. Envision a dynamic organization with a shared responsibility for student achievement that can adapt to changes in the environment.

2. Adhere to a set of core principles and beliefs, and communicate them consistently and clearly in multiple ways, from stories to slogans and over and over. Communicate face to face as much as possible. Maintain focus on learning for all students.

3. Focus on building the capacity of the system to learn at all levels. Invest in developing leaders of learning. Solicit feedback frequently and act on it.

4. Foster collaboration up, down, and across the system as a vehicle for continuous learning and shared accountability. Create intersecting learning communities so that everyone has ongoing access to professional support and learning. Ensure that purposes are clear and supports are in place.

5. Focus on a very small number of initiatives that clearly support one another and that can both build on and help develop shared conceptions about what it takes to improve learning. Build connections to what educators are already doing and what they are being asked to do differently. Tie

all initiatives to the fundamental goal of identifying and meeting the needs of each student.

6. Balance demands on educators with the supports they need in order to do what they are being asked to do (Marc Johnson, personal communication).

What is striking in this set of six principles is that this is a motion leader *explaining his approach to action.* It is clear, explicit, and oh-so-congruent with the leadership ideas that we have seen throughout this book. Furthermore, any one of our six leaders could have written these ideas. Even though these leaders are from all over the world and have never met, they would be entirely comfortable being in each other's shoes. Closer to peas in a pod than to chalk and cheese.

We see in Sanger a system in action in which coherence is fostered through purposeful learning and adjustments. What is especially characteristic about our motion leadership systems is that they extend learning from others: within the school, across schools, between the district and the schools, and with schools and districts in other locations. If your motion is confined to your own system, you will end up spinning your wheels.

Thus it becomes a natural extension for successful districts to want to extend their learning beyond their borders in a more organized fashion; hence, in this case, the formation of the California Office to Reform Education (CORE). While it doesn't address the needs of the whole state, CORE does represents nine districts, almost a quarter of the student population of the state (1.25 million out of 6 million). CORE grew out of a failed attempt to apply for the federal Race to the Top program. Its membership consists of the following districts: Clovis, Fresno, Long Beach, Los Angeles, Oakland, Sacramento, Sanger, and San Francisco.

Not all of the districts have been successful (Los Angeles, for example), but this mixture draws on a combination of savvy for getting success. Two features are especially noteworthy for successful districts like Sanger. They want to be part of a larger serious improvement enterprise for two reasons: This is their way of keeping on learning in order to sustain themselves, and they see it as a way of contributing their knowledge to others, thereby serving a larger moral purpose and in the process learning even more themselves. In other words, they are inclined to think bigger as they go.

The mission of each of the CORE districts and the collective is the same: increase student learning in high-poverty, high-minority, and high–English language learner student populations. The leaders of the member districts collaboratively seek solutions to shared challenges.

Echoing one of our leadership attributes for sustainability, Marc Johnson emphasizes that "whatever the size of the district, staying the course is perhaps the single most important contributor to long-term success." CORE also reflects that tendency of all good motion leaders: They naturally want to go bigger.

We don't know what will happen in the next couple of years in Sanger, but we can say that the district has greatly increased its chances of continuity by establishing a deeply shared culture of commitment and capacity to engage in ongoing improvement, and it has placed itself in a larger shared community of learners across eight districts where the push-and-pull of change requires them to learn from and contribute to the learning of other schools and systems. Finally, CORE itself may aspire to foster change within its own membership and beyond its borders in California.

Perhaps it is not necessary to say that if you can do all this in California, where the system is almost impossible to organize, it can be done anywhere.

ACT CUM VICTORIA

What lessons did Jim Watterston learn in his 3-year stint in ACT from 2009 to 2012, helping bring to life a somewhat coasting system? And what thinking does he bring to Victoria that represents a very different and more complex change challenge? Let's start in Canberra, where the government system of some 80 schools was somewhat stagnant in 2009. The challenge faced by Jim and his team involved stopping a decade-long decline in student numbers and a reduction of public confidence, lifting the performance of "coasting schools," improving overall performance in literacy and numeracy while reducing the gap between indigenous and nonindigenous students, increasing student retention rates in high school, and developing a stronger focus on early childhood learning.

By 2012 there was a lot of buy-in and good progress on most of the goals. How it was done will begin to sound familiar to readers of this book (although each story has its own context and nuances). In ACT Watterston started with his senior leadership team, signaling that there would be a shift from a school system where central control and school dependency was the norm to one where the work of teachers and schools was privileged by a responsive and better-aligned support system. As Jim put it, "The center now existed to serve schools, which was a challenging concept for many" central leaders. This very shift from bureaucratic hierarchy to grassroots involvement and partnership is virtually identical to what John Malloy is doing in Hamilton—with similar degrees of success in almost identical timelines of 3 years.

Jim established a new concept that he called "collaborative autonomy." Over a short period of time, school-level leaders embraced the belief that schools should be responsible for their own improvement, with the best way to get there being working with peers and in clusters to learn and achieve in teams (or, use the group to change the group strategy). Knowing also our communication findings (communication during implementation is paramount), Watterston delegated many of the management roles (finance and aspects of governance) and spent a large proportion of his time talking to stakeholders and experiencing firsthand the complexities of moving in the new direction.

It was at this stage that ACT's new corporate six principles emerged (see the list in Chapter 2). As this cultural change began to emerge, Watterston reinforced it with a structural change to support the new systemic beliefs. Note the sequence—cultural direction first, structure second. Most leaders do the reverse—change the structure and hope for a new culture (doesn't happen). The new structure consisted of organizing the system into four school networks of some 20 schools, each with a new school network leader (SNL).

These SNLs were to be coaches, provocateurs, and support brokers with the central office on behalf of each of the schools. A key part of the move involved appointing high-performing local principals to the SNL roles as a vote of confidence in ACT leadership, but also as a signal that a new form of leadership was on the rise.

This is a familiar refrain in our motion leadership cases—building new, concerted leadership capacity through development and new selection criteria, and setting off to do the new work of what I might call coordinated decentralization. But don't be misled by the word *decentralization*; there is very much a systemness quality to all of this as the coherent glue of common principles, mutual learning, camaraderie, and moral allegiance to the cause operates throughout the system. Incidentally, current emphasis on "school autonomy" in several jurisdictions can easily go wrong. It is not autonomy that is the goal, but rather *interdependence* (both laterally across schools and vertically between schools and the district or larger system; see Levin, 2012a). Local autonomy is just as much of a nonstarter for whole system reform as is top-down imposition.

In any case, in ACT Jim identifies four lessons (which, need I say, should sound familiar if you think of the other cases in this book):

1. Schools are built on relationships, and those connections and values need to be modeled from the top to the grassroots of the organization.

2. It is not enough to have a good plan; there needs to be full engagement, acceptance, and belief from the center and all stakeholders before it can succeed.

3. Investment is best made in building capacity of those closest to the point of delivery (i.e., teachers).

4. Improved policies and strategies work; simply asking people to do more does not!

After 3 years of "relentless focus" (another term that Jim uses), student numbers and retention have increased and ACT leads the nation in most testing categories. To be fair they were above average to begin with, but the point is that they have moved forward on almost all measures. Educators at all levels of the system will vouch for this success and, most important, they can explain *why* they are progressing. As I have said, motion leaders talk the walk as clearly as they walk the talk.

Melbourne is a different kettle of fish. But these are not the days of Alvarado moving from New York to California. Our change savvy is more known, and it includes the notion that, while each context is different, there are some common principles that need to take hold in every setting if we are to be successful. The new simplexity involves figuring out how to establish a set of strategies that are fit for the purpose in the new setting. And for Jim it is a much bigger system compared to ACT (some 2,200 schools from government, Catholic, and independent sectors vs. 84).

The situation in Victoria is intriguing for those of us interested in whole-system reform. For the past decade the previous government seemed to do all the right things for whole-system reform. There was great professional learning, a clear and evidence-based agenda, strong and motivating leadership at the center, and relatively strong buy-in by school leaders. In other words, the government did what I seem to be recommending in this book. It invested heavily in the right things, but the problem is that *progress was not forthcoming.* There was little improvement in student achievement; some schools have taken off, but many stagnated or moved backward.

We are not in a position to investigate why this happened (the usual suspects are lack of integrated coherence of the pieces, not enough intensity on implementation, and/or failure to obsess on student outcomes). The fact is it didn't work. And there is a new government with budget cuts to make and new aspirations to be pursued.

The government recently released a document called *Towards Victoria as a Learning Community* (Department of Education and Early Childhood Development, 2012b). Victoria has also just established a Strategic Plan for 2012–2016 (Department of Education, 2012a). It builds on the learning community document. I won't analyze it here, but let's say that it is a mixture of local autonomy and central direction. Its success will depend on a strong partnership that mobilizes sufficient sustained attention to actual implementation, which will not occur unless schools are learning from each other around a framed agenda. In other words, it will require the kind of motion leadership we are addressing in this book.

What Victoria has to do is create a more cohesive and engaging set of strategies in order to develop leaders and teachers who know what to do and how to do it with involved system direction as well as supportive tools and actions. They have to do what ACT did but on a much more complex and grand scale. We will want to keep a close eye on Victoria in the next while. It will be worth watching in order to derive new lessons about whole-system reform.

HACKNEY

Recall Richard Rumelt (2011) and his *good strategy, bad strategy.* In fact, he shows that most so-called strategy documents are not strategy at all but rather contain lofty goals and ambitions with no notion of what actions to take. He says that these plans lack ideas for *how* to get there. We are in luck with the Hackney case, because, guess what? Their self-claimed forte is precisely how to get improvement with the very diagnostic action combinations that will be required.

We know what Hackney did in the last decade, which is wonderfully documented by Alan Boyle and Salli Humphreys (2012) and which we summarized in Chapter 2. This London borough came from the bottom of the heap to end up above the national average on most measures of performance. They did it, they know what worked, and they can talk the walk with clarity and passion. Now, after being under the auspices of an external Learning Trust for the past 10 years, the system is returning to the municipality.

On August 1, 2012, the borough once again will be operating within the locally, democratically elected council of Hackney. Trish Okoruwa (a key school head, executive school head of a federation of five schools, and latterly deputy director of the Learning Trust) has been appointed as the new director of education in the new entity formally called Hackney Learning Trust. Her problem or challenge, as I mentioned earlier, is twofold: how to maintain and enhance the success trends across the borough, and how to do so in the immediate future under different and new governance.

Trish first summarizes what she thinks accounted for the success of the last 10 years: excellent appointments to the senior level of the organization; innovative models of school leadership, such as partnerships and federations; a real articulation of what *good* looks like; a focus on leadership of learning and the recruitment of the very best headteachers; and literacy as a key curriculum driver.

As part of the transition, Trish has led the effort to develop a new model for delivery of public sector services. She is on a relatively short leash because the new model is somewhat of a pilot trial, with a formal external evaluation to be conducted after 3 years.

Trish has already worked with school heads to develop the new model. It involves support for schools, with the center retaining intervention powers. They based their new model on the McKinsey report framework of how school systems go from adequate to good, to great, and to excellent (Mourshed, Chijoke, & Barber, 2010). They deem themselves as going from good or great to excellent, and to that end they have developed a performance tool that maps out the next steps for the system as a whole and where each school is on its own improvement journey.

Trish notes that they need to "up-skill" the education service workforce to be able to consistently deliver excellent service to each school. They are building in more peer review and corresponding intervention services. With budget cuts as the norm everywhere, Trish and her colleagues have set out a new 5-year vision. In her own words:

> We have defined what makes us successful, and it is our "how" [Rumelt cheering in the background]—the approach we take to delivering services and working in partnerships with our schools. This has been evidenced through a very much "action" approach to improvements—we are good at implementing and follow-through.

Always driven by the moral imperative realized, she adds, "We will champion the rights of parents and children to go to a good or outstanding school as a key driver."

Her strategy, developed over last few years, is to "predict and prevent," and "find and fix." The children in Hackney come from significant poverty backgrounds and diverse ethnic backgrounds. Like all of our cases, Hackney pays attention to outside research and practice. Trish stresses that they need to intervene as early as possible—find the kids and take action to fix problems. In addition to starting early, the new model also takes as a key point the entrance to secondary schools. Trish says:

> I have asked the secondary principals to start to dream a new dream—to use the predict-and-prevent strategy to support the young people at the point they enter secondary school, not to do excellent catch-up or revision work in their last year before they write the exams.

The 5-year plan can be downloaded from the Hackney website (www.learningtrust.co.uk), so I will just give a flavor of it to indicate especially the *action* or *how* part. There are nine sections to the plan:

1. Communicating our vision
2. Hackney Learning Trust
3. Championing excellence
4. School improvement
5. Early years
6. Fair admissions
7. Special education needs and disabilities
8. Vulnerable children
9. Adult learning

Perhaps not as skinny as our would-be motion leader might like, but the strength of the strategy, as I have said, is the focus on and clarity about *how*. Each of the nine areas has a simple *why, how,* and *what* focus. I will just take the first four to illustrate.

Vision

Why: defines our moral purpose and ambition for Hackney

How: defines the way we do things at Hackney and is the approach that differentiates us from competitors and makes us successful

What: defines what we do in practice to make the vision a reality

Hackney Learning Trust

Why: to improve the life chances of every child, young person, and adult learner in Hackney

How: driven by high ambition benchmark against the best; driven by measurable positive change and evidence; organizational focus is the quality of partner relationships; organization focus is the impact and effectiveness of delivery; cultivate intellectual capacity building in terms of knowledge, skills, and intelligence to improve what we do and how: cultivate innovation and accept risks

What: day-to-day, traded service; education outcomes and performance; continuous improvement plan

Championing Excellence

Why: raise achievement and aspiration so that all children experiences success regardless of where they live and their family background

How: engage national and international partners to identify excellence and innovate; develop and promote local models of leadership that build on the success of the best practitioners and federations; challenge and intervene to secure best governance and leadership in every school; promote a culture of high ambition and no excuses; develop and promote excellent practice in the pedagogy of teaching, learning, and assessment

What: disseminate national and international research to model excellence, briefings, conferences, and continuous professional learning; mediate the system through partnerships, sharing expertise across schools; identify and invest in growing leaders locally; lead the implementation of national policy change

School Improvement

Let's just take the *how*.

How: benchmark on best performance—not content with good enough; act quickly on detailed data and intelligence to provide school support; intervene speedily and rigorously to tackle poor or declining schools; promote innovation—development of teaching schools and information technology; develop expert capacity through partnerships working to help less-than-good schools

All and all, let's just say that it would be hard to go unnoticed in Hackney—for better or for worse!

Hackney is well aware that failed implementation is a result of not paying enough attention to the day-to-day *how* of getting things done. The *why* (purpose) and *what* (activities) are more obvious for most organizations, but it is the *how* of delivery where people slip up. Says Trish Okoruwa:

Describing the *how* is like describing our approach or the way of working and is the closest to being able to describe the culture and expectations within the organization. . . . Hence it is valuable for shaping the culture internally and equally valuable for communicating our approach externally in terms of a brand or value proposition that will sell our services or attract others to want to work in partnership with us. . . . Talking about how we do things and why our way is better is much easier to communicate and build on at every level of the organization.

Well, you get the picture. Hackney is deeply aware of the importance of the implementation stance. Hackney is a high-energy, high-focus system. They are exemplars of careful implementation and openness to learning new and better ways. In the past decade they have developed an enormous amount of motion leadership savvy. We will all be looking to see how they can develop this capacity even further. How far can skinny leaders go when they band together? Pay attention to Hackney in the next 3 years.

MOTION LEADERSHIP REDUX

If you refer back to Exhibit 3.5 as a checklist, you should have seen all of these attributes alive and well in action across the case examples. Proactive change stances that incorporate the seven elements were clear in ACT, Hamilton, Hackney, Park Manor, and Sanger. We frequently see references to the moral imperative, but less often do we see the kind of maniacal obsession to make sure it becomes realized in practice through whatever it takes. We see the mobilization of leadership, the related focus and relentless resolve to never let go of the goal.

It was probably less clear how impressive empathy plays its part, but none of the leaders took a cookie-cutter approach. They knew they had to get buy-in from diverse leaders, so they worked on what it would take to support them and entice them into the process that would enable these leaders to see their own goals fulfilled. The core group of leaders that I featured in this book certainly employed combinations of push, pull, and nudge. I hope you also saw how they all "thought bigger"—they worked on their own whole systems, but also each leader wanted to be plugged into the even bigger picture of helping and learning from others, finding out where in the world they could garner more ideas and evidence, and getting to know and possibly influence the state or national picture.

With respect to the implementation stance, these leaders were not going to leave anything to chance. They immersed themselves in the real excitement of accomplishment, always building capacity, avoiding complex plans, using data to pinpoint next moves, and mobilizing the group to change the group. By getting the group to be purposefully highly interactive, they ensured an organic pressure and support system that would be the envy of any bean counter.

These leaders were always planning ahead—for tomorrow, for next month and year, for the next few years, and then beyond when they knew they would no longer be around. They were going to stay the course as long as they were on duty. They knew that investing in ongoing leadership was crucial for today's impact, and at the same time was vital for the future—leaders developing leaders all the time. Finally, the reason that they could simultaneously field improvement and innovation was that they were preoccupied with evidence—what is working in our current work, what is going on in the rest of the world of education, what issues the system is concerned with including, what is on the horizon.

Motion leadership has got to be exciting. If we had an instrument to measure *irresistible engagement,* these leaders would be off the chart at the top end. Obstacles don't demoralize motion leaders. They are realists, except their realism has no upper limit. They respect the status quo in order to understand and transcend it—moral olympics. There really is no limit to what can be accomplished.

Someone once said the difference between an amateur and an expert is that the expert practices more. Motion leaders are always learning; that is how they stay skinny. There is no magic to motion leadership except the magical results. It really is simplexity—a small number of key elements (the simple part) and the wizardry of making these pieces gel in practice. When you participate as a lead learner, you actually do keep getting better. Be proud of your wisdom and humble about what you might not know. Of course, you don't know what you don't know, so you have to be ever vigilant about what new insights you might get.

There will be new things to discover as whole-system reform is now coming into urgent vogue. The new world will be more complex as I see right and wrong drivers coexisting in most places I go. There is not a state department of education or country that I could go into where capacity building is as much a part of the conversation as accountability. The arena has opened up but needs some serious sorting. Motion leaders pile on. You have a lot to contribute and a lot to learn; I can't think of a better job description.

This has been a short book—a skinny dip as it were. I hope it was bracing and embracing as well as exhilarating! The ultimate message is this: Grasp the meaning of the three stances and their attributes partly by reflecting on your own leadership experiences relative to the stances, but mainly by putting them into practice and learning therein.

EPILOGUE

IT HAS TO BE YOU!

We know what Marc Johnson, Trish Okoruwa, and Jim Watterston are facing as they enter new change situations. As experienced motion leaders they will also know to approach the challenges as a "use my knowledge while doubting what I know" proposition. They realize that they know a lot from their previous successes, but they also know they will learn more in each new setting, enabling them to hone the skinny of change.

But what about you, the reader? Leadership is the central resource for all improvements—leaders who develop themselves as they develop others. In the 21st century, to survive, it is getting to the point where *everyone* needs to think of themselves as a leader of their own destiny, and as we have made it clear you better hitch your destiny to others in a collective effort to make things better for yourself and others.

Leaders within education have a special, timely responsibility. The current system is just about bankrupt, with increased boredom of students and alienation of teachers. But it is worse than that. In some countries (the United States, for one), *the price of inequality* (the gap between the very rich 1% and the remaining 99%) is growing in leaps and bounds. As Joseph Stiglitz (2012) puts it, this is leading inexorably to Armageddon. This is not simply a matter of the rich getting richer. Virtually everyone—99%—is becoming worse off, more and more of them desperately so. Education is probably the most powerful force that could intervene to alter the direction. For that to happen we will need scores of motion leaders.

The exciting news is that we are on the ground floor of fundamental, disruptive innovations that have enormous power to do good. Pedagogical partnerships between and among students and teachers are now a distinct possibility, if we can integrate technology and new learning and use our change knowledge (Fullan, 2013). If we lead it well, we can accomplish great gains in learning for all in fairly short order. We will need leaders who can think and do bigger as we have seen in this book.

Review the success stories in this book; use the three motion leadership stances—change, implementation, and sustainability—as a checklist. Commit to being your own motion leader, causing positive movement in your own place and remembering that it is a collective sport. You can't really improve yourself without improving others, and vice versa. Go big and take others with you.

We have seen in this book, through the actions of several leaders in diverse settings, what the skinny of change looks like. You now know enough to lead with improvement wherever you are on the leadership scale or on the world scale. You have no excuse for not developing your own skinny of change leadership. Ah, but we always have Fr. Egsgard to test our limits. Do you want to put in the effort to become a good change agent, a very good one, or a great one? According to Fr. Egsgard, the choice is yours!

REFERENCES

Bajak, F. (2012, July 3). Peru's ambitious laptop program gets mixed grades. *Associated Press.* Retrieved from http://bigstory.ap.org/article/perus-ambitious-laptop-program-gets-mixed-grades

Barber, M., Donnelley, K., & Saad, R. (2012). *Oceans of innovation: The Atlantic, the Pacific, global leadership and the future of education.* London, UK: The Institute of Public Policy Research.

Boyle, A., & Humphreys, S. (2012). *A revolution in a decade: Ten out of ten.* London, UK: Leannta.

Department of Education and Early Childhood Development. (2012a). *DEECD 2012–2016 Strategic Plan.* Melbourne, Australia: Author.

Department of Education and Early Childhood Development. (2012b). *Towards Victoria as a learning community.* Melbourne, Australia: Author.

Fullan, M. (1982). *The meaning of educational change* (4th ed.). New York, NY: Teachers College Press.

Fullan, M. (2007). *The new meaning of educational change.* New York, NY: Teachers College Press.

Fullan, M. (2010). *All systems go.* Thousand Oaks, CA: Corwin.

Fullan, M. (2011a). *Choosing the wrong drivers for whole system reform.* Policy paper 204. Melbourne, Australia: Centre for Strategic Education.

Fullan, M. (2011b). *Moral imperative realized.* Thousand Oaks, CA: Corwin.

Fullan, M. (2013). *Stratosphere: Integrating technology, pedagogy, and change knowledge.* Toronto, Ontario, Canada: Pearson Canada.

Hackney Learning Trust. *5 year vision for education in Hackney 2012–2017.* London, UK: Author.

Hargreaves, A., & Braun, H. (2012). *Leading for all: Final report of the review of the development of Essential for Some, Good for*

All—Ontario's strategy for special education reform devised by the Council of Directors of Education. Toronto, Ontario, Canada: Council of Directors of Education.

Hargreaves, A., & Fullan, M. (2012). *Professional capital: Transforming teaching in every school.* New York, NY: Teachers College Press.

Hargreaves, A., & Shirley, D. (2012). *The global fourth way.* Thousand Oaks, CA: Corwin.

Hattie, J. (2012). *Visible learning for teachers.* London, UK: Routledge.

Hopper, K., & Hopper, W. (2007). *The puritan gift: Triumph, collapse and revival of an American dream.* London, UK: I. B. Taurus.

Institute for Educational Leadership. (2012). *Ontario leadership framework (2012).* Retrieved from http://www.education-leadership-ontario.ca/content/framework

Leana, C. (2011). The missing link in school reform. *Stanford Social Innovation Review, 9*(4), 30–35.

Levin. B. (2012a). *Interdependence, not autonomy, is the key.* Nottingham, UK: National College of Leadership.

Levin, B. (2012b). *More high school graduates.* Thousand Oaks, CA: Corwin.

Levin, B. (2012c). *System-wide improvement in education.* Paris, France: UNESCO and the International Academy of Education.

Liker, J., & Meier, D. (2007). *Toyota talent.* New York, NY: McGraw-Hill.

Machiavelli, N. (2007). *The prince.* New York, NY: Vintage Press. (Original work published 1532)

Martinez, A., Diaz, D., & Aloso, S. (2009). *First national monitoring and evaluation report on Plan Ceibal.* Montevideo, Uruguay: Monocromo.

Mourshed, M., Chijoke, C., & Barber, M. (2010). *How the world's most improved systems keep getting better.* London, UK: McKinsey.

New York City Excellence Commission. (2012). *New York City Excellence Commission: Terms of reference.* New York, NY: Author.

Ontario Ministry of Education. (2012). *Ontario leadership framework.* Toronto, Ontario, Canada: Author.

Organisation for Economic Co-operation and Development. (2010). *PISA 2009 results: Learning trends, Volume 5.* Paris: Author.

Pfeffer, J., & Sutton, R. I. (2006). *Hard facts, dangerous half-truths, and total nonsense: Profiting from evidence-based management.* Boston, MA: Harvard Business School.

Ravitch, D. (2010). *The death and life of the great American school system: How testing and choice are undermining education.* New York, NY: Basic Books.

Reeves, D. B. (2009). *Leading change in your school: How to conquer myths, build commitment, and get results.* Alexandria, VA: Association for Supervision and Curriculum Development.

Reeves, D. B. (2011). *Finding your leadership focus: What matters most for student results.* New York, NY: Teachers College Press.

Regional Bureau for Sciences in Latin America and the Caribbean. (2011). *Plan Ceibal in Uruguay: From pedagogical reality to an ICT roadmap for the future.* Montevideo, Uruguay: UNESCO.

Robinson, V. (2011). *Student centered leadership.* San Francisco, CA: Jossey-Bass.

Rumelt, R. (2011). *Good strategy and bad strategy.* New York, NY: Crown Business.

Sharratt, L., & Fullan, M. (2012). *Putting FACES on the data.* Thousand Oaks, CA: Corwin.

Stiglitz, J. (2012). *The price of inequality.* New York, NY: W. W. Norton & Sons.

Thaler, R., & Sunstein, C. (2008). *Nudge: Improving decisions about health, wealth, and happiness.* New Haven, CT: Yale University Press.

Wagner, T. (2012). *Creating innovators: The making of young people who will change the world.* New York, NY: Simon & Schuster.

INDEX

CORWIN

A SAGE Company

The Corwin logo—a raven striding across an open book—represents the union of courage and learning. Corwin is committed to improving education for all learners by publishing books and other professional development resources for those serving the field of PreK–12 education. By providing practical, hands-on materials, Corwin continues to carry out the promise of its motto: **"Helping Educators Do Their Work Better."**

ONTARIO PRINCIPALS' COUNCIL

Exemplary Leadership in Public Education

The Ontario Principals' Council (OPC) is a voluntary association for principals and vice-principals in Ontario's public school system. We believe that exemplary leadership results in outstanding schools and improved student achievement. To this end, we foster quality leadership through world-class professional services and supports. As an ISO 9001 registered organization, we are committed to **"quality leadership—our principal product."**

learningforward

Advancing professional learning for student success

Learning Forward (formerly National Staff Development Council) is an international association of learning educators committed to one purpose in K–12 education: Every educator engages in effective professional learning every day so every student achieves.